"This volume goes beyond theory in providing many illuminating examples that can be replicated with considerable practical hands-on wisdom about fundraising. Bravo!"

Barry Z. Posner, PhD, Michael J. Accolti, S.J. Professor of Leadership, Santa Clara University

"Contributors tell their stories passionately and jargon free, making this an engaging book accessible to the professional and layperson alike."

Dennis Conroy, Senior Vice President, External Affairs, Metropolitan Family Services, Chicago

"I truly loved the book and found it to be so very Vincentian, grounded in tradition, simple and straightforward, organized and practical. I will be using it."

James D Davis, RN, Consultant, Mission and Ethics, Seton Family of Hospitals

"This is a book about fundraising—by Vincentians—for Vincentians. It founds our search for funds in our spiritual roots while providing practical, actually-used fundraising methods by United States Vincentians across the Family."

Sheila Gilbert, President National Council of the United States Society of St. Vincent de Paul

"This short, easy-to-read book is both inspirational and practical. From Vincent, the reader learns three valuable insights that are as relevant today as they were 400 years ago: Respect donors; prepare fundraisers to understand that this work is a sacred ministry; and reverence the recipients."

Georgette Lehmuth, OSF, President and CEO, National Catholic Development Conference

"This ground-breaking new work offers a comprehensive overview of the complexity of charitable fundraising. This book melds what Vincent de Paul called the "practical and the possible," with case studies and stories from dedicated and experienced people in this field."

G. Gregory Gay, C.M., Superior General, Congregati

"This book is a stimulating and useful resource for fundr social conscience….a serendipitous collection of practica motivated by compassion and service."

Joseph McCann, C.M., PhD, Professor Emeritus, St. Patrick's College & Al

Fundraising Strategies
Stories from the Field
Inspired by St. Vincent de Paul

Fundraising Strategies
Stories from the Field
Inspired by St. Vincent de Paul

EDITED BY
PATRICIA M. BOMBARD, B.V.M.
J. PATRICK MURPHY, C.M.

VINCENT ON LEADERSHIP: THE HAY PROJECT

DE PAUL UNIVERSITY
COLLEGE OF LIBERAL ARTS
AND SCIENCES
School of Public Service

Fundraising Strategies—Stories from the Field Inspired by St. Vincent de Paul
Published by Vincent on Leadership: The Hay Project,
School of Public Service, DePaul University

© 2015 Vincent on Leadership: The Hay Project
All rights reserved.
Printed in the United States of America.

www.vincentianfundraising.org

First Edition

Paperback ISBN-13: 978-1514367544

To William (Bill) Hay and Mary Pat Gannon Hay in recognition of their many generous charitable endeavors.

To all those who through the centuries have continued to respond with heart and hands to the Vincentian question "What must be done?"

And to all those we seek to serve.

Acknowledgments

WE could not have undertaken the creation of this book without the generous response by the chapter authors to our invitation to write the story of their organization and their hard-won lessons around resource development and sustainability. We respect and admire all of them for the way they embody Vincentian values and ideals, and for the way they inspire many others and us.

We are deeply grateful to William (Bill) Hay and Mary Pat Gannon Hay, whose generous donation to DePaul University allowed us to launch Vincent on Leadership: The Hay Project, with its mission of codifying Vincent's leadership legacy and enhancing the leadership of Vincentians around the world.

We also thank two people without whose help this book would not look the way it does today: Carol Hohle, our consultant and book designer, and Laura Matthews, our editor.

Contents

Introduction
The Story Is Vincent

I cannot tell you how much alms have diminished here and the
difficulty of finding any loans. Everyone is being affected
by the misery of the age.
—Vincent de Paul

YOU MAY BE asking yourself, "Do I need to read another book on
nonprofit fundraising?" Simply stated, our answer is, "Yes—this
one."

There are two reasons we make this claim. First, the wisdom and practical tips you will read in this book are time-tested. How much time are we
talking about? Nearly 400 years. This book demonstrates the leadership
legacy of St. Vincent de Paul (1581–1660), who began life as the son of
a peasant farmer and ended up sowing seeds of a different kind—a work
others continue today. The Catholic Patron Saint of Charity, Vincent
founded his first organization to offer service to the poor in France in
1617. His organizational and management brilliance were such that this
organization, known in the United States as the Ladies of Charity, still
exists today. Vincent said, "The poor suffer less from a lack of generosity
than from a lack of organization." He set about to correct that by organizing the first systematic approaches to social service.

Second, we are convinced you will be inspired by what you read here to recommit yourself to the work you already are doing to be of service and to create your own legacy. In these pages are never-before-told stories of Vincentian organizations around the world, run by people who follow Vincent's maxim: "It is not enough to do good, it must be done well." In addition to the Ladies of Charity, those organizations include the Congregation of the Mission (Vincentian priests and brothers), the Daughters of Charity, the Society of Saint Vincent de Paul, Depaul International, and many other organizations worldwide.

There are more than 1,500 biographies written about Vincent de Paul. This is the only book written about raising resources that support the mission to serve the poor that he launched long ago.

How to Read This Book

Our intention in creating this book is to help you be better at what you are already doing. How that happens is largely up to you and the degree to which you put what is here into practice in your own life and organization.

At the end of each chapter are some discussion questions. We hope you will use these with your team to spark conversation on how to lead change and improvements in your own organization.

In Chapter 1, authors Steve Martinez and Roger Playwin explain the comprehensive, time-tested, and personalized Vincentian approach to helping individuals in need through the story of the St. Vincent de Paul Society's response to Hurricane Katrina.

In Chapter 2, John Rybolt, C.M., a noted Vincentian scholar, explores the enduring nature of Vincent's legacy. People who know his story admire Vincent for his extraordinary ability to connect both rich and poor to his mission. The author offers behavioral examples of Vincent's transparency and responsibility to donors.

Chapter 3 tells the history and present activities of the Ladies of Charity, the oldest of Vincent's organizations. This international organization will celebrate its four-hundredth anniversary in 2017.

2

In Chapter 4, Mark Pranaitis encourages nonprofit leaders to go after major and planned gifts. This encouragement, says Pranaitis, is rooted in Vincent's call to not only serve the poor, but to do it well.

In Chapter 5, you'll read about young Vincentians in Denver, Colorado. As explained by the group's founders Mary Frances and Bill Jaster, the Colorado Vincentian Volunteers is about providing resources and support for young people who want to give a year of service.

Chapter 6 offers practical advice on talking with donors about how their relationship with your organization's mission can continue even after death. The author, Vincentian priest Charles Shelby, has decades of experience in the area of planned giving and speaks frankly about its challenges and rewards.

In Chapter 7, you will meet Bill and Mary Pat Gannon Hay, two contemporary examples of how the Vincentian legacy has inspired extraordinary service, commitment, and the very tangible giving of self and financial resources.

Chapter 8 tackles one of the most difficult aspects of fundraising: moving beyond rejection. Author Teresa Manna first recognizes its emotional impact. Then, using examples from her own and others' experiences, she helps us to move beyond the emotion and "reveal the redeeming value of rejection."

In Chapter 9, the authors Mark McGreevy and Lianne Howard-Dace tell the story of how Depaul International has grown from a $300,000 per year charity founded 25 years ago in England to one that today raises $30,000,000 annually and has an international presence. Depaul demonstrates Vincent's timeless appeal and his mandate to be creative to infinity.

In Chapter 10, J. Patrick Murphy illustrates several practical, alternative sources of revenue for nonprofits, including examples of Vincent-inspired organizations creating modern streams of revenue for their mission.

Even as Pope Francis today is renewing the Catholic Church by emphasizing its original mission to care for the poor and reforming the Roman Curia from the inside, St. Vincent de Paul reformed the church of France from the inside by educating and forming the clergy. This book's authors offer a great deal of wisdom and insight about Vincent and fundraising from their experience—practitioners writing from the heart about the good being done in Vincent's name 400 years after he launched his organizations to serve the poor.

1

Disaster Preparedness
A Vincentian Response to Katrina

STEVEN F. MARTINEZ AND ROGER PLAYWIN

Doing good isn't everything; it must be done well.
—Vincent de Paul

It's easy to remember the headlines: "Death..." "Destruction..." "Complete Devastation..." "Catastrophic..." "Under Water..." "Millions Stranded..." "Gone—We Lost Everything." Iconic visuals showed the New Orleans Superdome's thin roof ripped off. Thousands of people were stranded inside, running out of water and food, with no place to sleep, no police to maintain order, no plan for evacuation, and family members missing.

In August 2005, Hurricane Katrina, the most destructive storm ever to strike the United States, hit the Southeast. It is hard to envision the power of such a storm—a Category 3 hurricane, with winds reaching 140 mph, 100-foot waves, and a storm surge more than twenty-eight feet high. The storm caused an unprecedented devastation along the coasts of Louisiana, Alabama, and Mississippi, covering more than 90,000 square miles (the size of Great Britain). Eighty percent of New Orleans was under water. Water as deep as twenty feet flooded major roads, bridges, homes, office buildings, highways, and airports. More than 1.7 million people lost power in the Gulf States and another 1.3 million were similarly affected in Florida. Damage estimates for Hurricane Katrina topped $75 billion, making it the most costly hurricane in history.

Being prepared for disaster is one of the most crucial reasons nonprofits must do all they can to be fully funded and optimally organized around core values.

It's times like these that make the more mundane efforts at fundraising so critically important. Being prepared for disaster is one of the most crucial reasons nonprofits must do all they can to be fully funded and optimally organized around core values. With those elements firmly established, it is possible to spring into action at a moment's notice.

Vincentians Respond to Katrina

Members of the Society of St. Vincent de Paul—or "Vincentians"—strive to grow spiritually by offering person-to-person service to individuals in need. Consequently, the Society of Saint Vincent de Paul (SVdP) responded to Katrina on all levels within its organizational structure.

Chaos ensued immediately after this horrific event. The sheer volume of calls for assistance and of individuals showing up on local SVdP office doorsteps was overwhelming. Katrina tested the channels of communication within the organization as well as the character of its members.

> When you have lost everything except the clothes on your back, you can only pray and ask God to direct you to where there is hope. I found that hope at the Society of Saint Vincent de Paul Katrina Aid Assistance Program. (Hurricane Katrina evacuee, *Response to Katrina*, p. 113.)

The Vincentians' response was deeply embedded in the founding Vincentian Principles of the Society. These principles guide the spirituality of the Vincentians and have a dramatic effect on the manner in which Vincentians respond to people seeking assistance.

St. Vincent de Paul (1581–1660), a Catholic priest and a man of deep faith, keen intellect, and enormous creativity, has become known as the "The Apostle of Charity" and "Father of the Poor." His contributions to the training of priests and organizing parish missions and other services for the poor shaped the Catholic Church's role in the modern world. Vincent's lifework was to bring together for-profit, nonprofit and government sectors to serve the poor. He provided leadership, vision, problem-solving skills, and love to attract countless people into service.

"We must do what is agreeable to God."

The codification of Vincentian principles of service to the poor as an expression of Christ trace back to 1833, when Frederic Ozanam and six college students defined the organizational values that became the basis for SVdP. These core values frame SVdP's vocation, values, spirituality, prayers, rule, and mission. Ozanam's vision inspired the Vincentian movement to expand into an international charity network. He wrote, "We must do what is agreeable to God. Therefore, we must do what our Lord Jesus Christ did when preaching the gospel. Let's go to the poor!" SVdP was established on this vision (*Manual*, p. 9).

Vincentians are called to a vocation, an intimate desire to participate in helping the needy through person-to-person contact and a desire for spiritual growth as found in service to the suffering and poor. Vincentians are women and men who seek personal holiness by providing direct assistance to the poor through food, clothing, housing, medical goods, and other forms of aid. People from every ethnic and cultural background, age group, and economic level honor this calling. The deep inner belief that guides Vincentians is the commitment to treating all individuals with dignity, compassion, and respect. This commitment has lasted for centuries and spread around the world.

Organizational Structure a Good Foundation

No single organization could have been completely prepared to meet all the needs created by Hurricane Katrina. However, the structure of the SVdP provided an effective channel for responding to local disasters. Local SVdP actions involved much more than the typical Vincentian response to a more limited disaster (such as a home fire or flood). According to its bylaws, the Society of Saint Vincent de Paul National Council (SVdPUSA) provides disaster-relief services. It has a standing disaster-services committee and is authorized to provide assistance under the Stafford Emergency and Disaster Assistance Act. Authorizing the U.S. president to make emergency declarations that trigger aid from 28 federal agencies and outside organizations, this act also created the Federal Emergency Management Agency (FEMA) and gives it authority to recognize relief and disaster-assistance organizations (nonprofits authorized to provide disaster assistance).

Until Katrina, the SVdP had never been called on to provide services under the Stafford Act. Once Katrina struck, however, SVdP received authorization to assist relief efforts through a memorandum of understanding and other agreements with volunteer organizations and governmental agencies. The services provided by SVdP included emergency shelter, mental health services, health services, first aid, medical assistance, food service, social services for basic needs, and services to volunteers.

The SVdP identified 606 of its 4,500 U.S. regional units or "conferences" as heavily affected by Katrina. Shreveport, Biloxi, and Baton Rouge were in the direct path of the storm. The relocation of 1.9 million people strained many conferences beyond these states.

Michael Acaldo, executive director of Baton Rouge SVdP, said, "We were working here before the hurricane. We are an organization with no red tape or bureaucracy. We are where the rubber meets the road. We are here with food and clothing, all the necessities to make a difference in the life of someone who may have lost everything" (*Response to Katrina,* p. 12).

The Baton Rouge Conference, which usually provided 13,000 meals at one location, found itself serving 43,300 meals at various locations throughout the community. In the first few weeks after the storm, the conference distributed 150,000 articles of clothing to more than 31,000 people through the local SVdP thrift store. Trucks delivered loads of crucial goods such as water, diapers, clothing, food, furniture, appliances, and medications.

A testament to how Vincentians responded was captured in the Hurricane Katrina Case #11 Report (*Response to Katrina,* p. 73): "The house [the Katrina victims] were living in had no furniture, chairs, beds, or appliances. Their assessment was completed while sitting on the bare floor. Within days, Vincentians were able to secure beds for all the family members and, in partnership with a local church, secured a stove, refrigerator, washer, and dryer."

In the aftermath of Hurricane Katrina, requests for assistance flooded the SVdP local conferences. Stretched beyond their normal capacity, the conferences looked to the next level of the organization, SVdP councils, for help. Councils routinely operate autonomously in disasters, but because of the far-reaching devastation and the large number of evacuees transported into many different council areas, they, too, were overwhelmed. Evacuees were transported directly to safe areas with nothing but the clothes on their backs. Many were separated from family members, creating the need for a system of communications throughout the SVdP and other first responders.

Six of eight SVdP regions were overwhelmed. In just one month, for instance, Houston served more than 51,000 individuals; received more than 800 daily calls; and provided $3 million in food, clothing, and medical supplies. Baton Rouge served more than 50,000 and provided 170,000 items of clothing. In Atlanta, the SVdP served 18,000 people, spending more than $1.7 million for basic materials for evacuees. San Antonio served more than 25,000 individuals. In a brief period after Katrina, SVdP councils across the country had served more than 125,000 survivors, providing food, clothing, medical supplies, and logging more than 32,000 volunteer hours.

Creation of the National Disaster Relief Coordinator

The regional structure quickly became overloaded. The national council of the SVdP sprang into action, creating the temporary position of national disaster relief coordinator. This position was responsible for expediting communications about unmet needs of disaster victims, coordinating resources, and formulating optimal practices even while supporting the autonomy of local councils. This proved invaluable, as the national office fielded huge volumes of calls each day seeking money, food, water, and clothing.

The coordinator had extensive experience as the chairman of disaster operations for the American Red Cross in the St. Louis region. He knew what needed to be done and was able to accomplish it quickly. He first executed a memorandum of understanding with FEMA. His methodology was introduced in the SVdP chapters across the country, showing how they could take leadership roles as strategic partners in providing disaster relief and establishing the SVdP as an "official relief organization." This also encouraged federal approval for support services with a connection to a stream of income to assist with basic emergency services.

The SVdP national council fielded thousands of calls and coordinated the distribution of millions of dollars of in-kind items to councils across the country. For example, an anonymous donor offered truckloads of household "set up packages" (beds, linens, kitchenware, dressers, tables, and more). These items were high priority but also created a challenge, since the SVdP conferences and councils were already overwhelmed. The disaster coordinator identified open SVdP warehouse space throughout the SVdP and brokered the donation. With precision, tractor-trailers filled with supplies (valued at $3.5 million) delivered goods from across the country to the disaster's front lines. The donor was so impressed with the SVdP's abilities, he made a second donation—valued at $4 million—for distribution by the SVdPUSA national disaster coordinator.

The donor was so impressed,
he made a second donation.

The coordinator signed a letter of agreement with Matthew 25 Ministries (M25M)—an international Christian humanitarian relief organization known for helping the poorest of the poor—to provide containers and semi-trailers of materials and supplies to meet basic needs.

In response to the outcry for case management services across the country and the vast experience of SVdP Vincentians in conducting person-to-person evaluations over the last 160 years, the national disaster coordinator submitted a grant proposal to the United Methodist Committee on Relief (UMCOR) for national case management services. Fifteen SVdP councils participated.

A selling point to UMCOR was SVdP's national network of 4,100 parish-based conferences and 451 diocesan and district councils that could further enhance the goals of this project. The grant provided $6 million, and SVdPUSA generated an additional $8.3 million of in-kind contributions.

Finally, the SVdP national disaster coordinator secured a state-of-the-art mobile kitchen called Hope, a commercial-grade kitchen capable of serving 10,000 people per day. Walter McKenna, CFO of Specialty Brands of America, made the donation. Built at a cost of more than

$400,000, the national board of the SVdP received the asset, and it is now available to respond to emergency disasters of any kind.

Motivated by Spiritual Growth

What did we at SVdP learn from Vincentian responses to this large-scale disaster?

First, while the SVdP structure is readily able to handle smaller local disasters, the conferences and councils can be easily overwhelmed in larger emergencies. In large-scale disasters, regional support is limited to being a communication channel. By far the smartest strategy was the temporary hiring of the national disaster coordinator. This was key in creating a single point for communications, donations, and distributions.

To encourage growth and readiness, organizations must emphasize core values.

Second, and most importantly, the Vincentian response was a testament to the importance of the founding Vincentian principles given to the SVdP by Ozanam and practiced by Vincent himself. To continue the growth and readiness of the SVdP, conferences and councils must emphasize core values and "Vincentian formation."

Vincentians are better equipped to meet overwhelming needs quickly and efficiently because of common core values and their experience acting on these values. These values enable volunteers to persevere through extreme conditions, to provide customary face-to-face assistance with dignity, and to reassure survivors that their basic needs will be met and they will be able to put their lives back together. A Vincentian, in her Katrina report to the National Council, said it best: "It's been crazy, because I haven't had a day off. I went from working two days to working two weeks straight, but it's all for a good reason, a good cause. We are going the extra mile to see they get what they need!" (*Response to Katrina*, p. 13).

Vincentians have been practicing these fundamental principles for centuries. They meet face-to-face with those in need, exploring how to best address every need. Vincentians also strive to grow spiritually, always moving toward holiness, much like Frederic Ozanam and Vincent de Paul approached their own works. This approach is the SVdP's distinguishing feature among disaster-relief workers. Vincentians are known for working until the job is done—regular people called to perform extraordinary tasks.

"Why are you working over the forty hours required by FEMA?" a FEMA employee asked a Vincentian. SVdP executive director Liz Disco Shearer answered, "Vincentians work the 40 hours as requested by FEMA, but also donate another 30 hours to help with God's work."

A recipient said later, "God's love was shown to me through you. God's word said, 'When I was hungry, you fed me. When I was naked, you clothed me.' As for me, when I needed you to listen, you were there. When I needed a hug, you were there. When I needed you to care, you gave all you had. My family wants to say thank you from the bottom of our hearts, to you and the Society of St. Vincent de Paul" (*Response to Katrina*, p. 121).

Questions for Discussion

1. Vincent "loved to use this succinct motto: *Totum opus nostrum in operatione consistit* (Action is our entire task)" (Pujo, 251). What were one or two key actions of the SVdP after Katrina that illustrate Vincent's motto?

2. What are one or two key ways our organization can be more action-focused in the manner of Vincent de Paul? What about in our own lives?

3. What is our normal response time with clients? What about in emergencies? How do we rise to the challenge?

2
Vincent de Paul as a Fundraiser
His Attitudes and Practices

JOHN E. RYBOLT, C.M.

We should assist the poor in every way
and do it both by ourselves and by enlisting the help of others.
—Vincent de Paul

IN THE Parisian church of St. Sulpice, a side chapel is dedicated to
St. Vincent de Paul. He had worked there with the founder of the
Society of St. Sulpice, Jean-Jacques Olier, for some years and assisted
him on his deathbed. One of the painted elements in the ceiling of the
chapel shows Vincent in a gesture unique to this chapel. He is seated
and turns away in horror from a richly dressed man standing before him,
undoubtedly someone asking a favor in return for some financial consideration. This image reflects the common understanding about Vincent's
fundraising: he never indulged in any kind of corrupt practice, which was
widely accepted in the patronage society of his time. Exactly what event
the image refers to is unknown, but it reflects his incorruptibility and
freedom from personal benefit.

Fundraising is a new area of study relative to religious organizations. Except for periods of close relationship with civil governments, religious organizations (dioceses, religious communities, and charitable institutions of all sorts) were independent of them, such as in the earliest days of the Church and in more recent times. As a result they had to depend on the goodwill offerings of benefactors. One of the standard complaints of religious leaders has been their lack of people and money. Unfortunately, the drive toward financial support entailed practices that became corrupt over the years, such as clergy accepting payment to arrange for supposed heavenly forgiveness. This managed to alienate the faithful in many places. Calls for reform, concerning dogma and pastoral practice, as well as finances, reverberated throughout the Church by Vincent's time (1581–1660), leading to a search for best practices.

In this chapter, I have chosen to include mainly unpublished materials previously overlooked by others. Why were they unpublished? Pierre Coste and his predecessor Jean-Baptiste Pémartin omitted from their collection of Vincentian texts many that they found to be too secular and lacking in what they decided was spirituality. That decision kept generations of Vincentians from knowing authentic and interesting texts that give deep insight into the daily life of their mentor.

As to the methodology, I have attempted to uncover both what Vincent did and why. Examining these methods and attitudes demonstrates not only how he related to those he invited to finance good works but also to the recipients of this support. One caution should be made at the beginning, however. A simple solution to the issue of Vincent's fundraising would be to impose contemporary best practices on his period and then look for similarities between the two periods, ours and his, to illustrate a point. Instead, we need to let the texts speak for themselves, allowing us to draw the lessons of wisdom for today from the experience of the past.

Context

Colin Jones, the British commentator on relief for European poor in St. Vincent's period, pointed to the "charitable imperative" of the Catholic reformation (Grell/Cunningham, p. 13).

To take an active role in the care of the poor came to be a sign of a renewed Catholic.

Under pressure of the Wars of Religion, in Britain the crown gained control of relief for the poor along with hospitals from the munici-palities (of whatever confession) and found itself competing with a revitalized Catholic Church. Jones sees here what he calls a "charitable imperative"—a moral obligation to give. To take an active role in the care of the poor came to be a sign of a renewed Catholic, seeking to put into practice an *imitatio Christi* (the imitation of Christ). The ideology of renewed Catholicism was also crucial to developments in health care and relief for the poor in France.

It was precisely here that we see Vincent operating. He shared the same general sense about the social condition as did his acquaintance and near contemporary Antoine Godeau (1605–1672), bishop of Grasse. Speaking from the perspective of his theological background, Godeau's exhortation to do charitable works was founded on a concept of atone-ment: "From whence come these changes [the social disorder of the early 1650s]? From the war; and what has lit the fire [of conflict]? What has fed [this conflict] for the last twenty years? Your sins. Thus atone for your sins through your acts of charity" (McHugh, pp. 35–36). Vincent de Paul's expressions were less stark than Godeau's, but both he and the bishop were interested in the same project—relief for the poor in devastated provinces.

Another of Vincent's contemporaries was Charles Maignart de Bernières (1616–1662) (Féron). It was he who developed the practice of gathering the reports from the Vincentians dispatched to serve the poor in the provinces of Picardy and Champagne and then publishing these reports in increasing quantities for distribution around France. Their purpose was to advertise the needs of the poor. Although Vincent did not publish Maignart's reports personally, he did use them to motivate the Ladies of Charity—the Parisian noblewomen who organized to serve the poor—and to direct the apportioning of the funds received.

One family that strongly felt the influence of this "charitable imperative" was the Bretonvilliers. The matriarch of the family, Claude-Elisabeth, opened areas of her large Parisian mansion on the Île Saint-Louis for the storage of goods collected in the capital. Charity so marked her family that her son Alexandre joined the Society of St. Sulpice, and Vincent de Paul presided at his installation in 1657 as their second superior general.

Attitudes

Vincent's leading attitude toward relief for the poor was the sacredness of the task. This guided his attempts in his own life, as will be seen below, as well as in his relations with possible donors. His work was to sensitize them, as he was sensitized, to the inner meaning of what they were doing.

Vincent's leading attitude toward relief for the poor was the sacredness of the task.

As is well known, Vincent strove throughout his long priestly life to be aware of the presence of God. Being faced with so many poor and suffering, which had increased in Europe during his lifetime, must have caused him to reflect deeply on the meaning of their presence. He embraced an ancient perspective: to see the suffering Jesus in the person of the poor. Others saw the poor as a problem that should be excised from society. Vincent, however, was countercultural in seeing his poor and ignorant brothers and sisters as emblematic of Jesus himself. Since the Church's teaching is that all Christians form one body with their Savior, Vincent believed that if any one of them suffered, it was incumbent on the others to relieve their distress as they would for Christ.

Vincent was able to focus on this theological perspective because he had plenty of time to reflect on it. He rarely missed his daily hour of morning meditation, and the insights he gained in prayerful reflection helped guide that day's thoughts and actions.

When speaking to his fellow priests, he referenced the inspiration he received in his meditative reading of the Scriptures. One example is his explication of Jeremiah 35:1–11, which includes an account of the Rechabites, a group of counter-cultural tribespeople who maintained the ancient form of life of pastoral nomads. Vincent presented them as examples of those who relied in a radical way on divine providence (provision) alone. "The fact remains that the trust of this man [Rechab] was so great that he deprived himself of all the conveniences of life to depend absolutely on the care of Providence" (Conf. to CM 198, CCD, 12:118). In an unpublished conference address on the same topic, Vincent exclaimed:

> Oh, *mon Dieu*, my brothers, let us ask of the divine goodness a perfect confidence in his province, since, provided we are faithful to God, we will lack nothing. . . . Oh, the misery of the one who dares to rely more on his own work than on the goodness of God. . . . Let us take our rest in the loving care of a God who watches over our needs and whose wisdom is infinite. Let us think only about serving him well. (Lyons manuscript, p. 274r.)

Practices

Vincent's theological attitudes, prayerfully considered, guided his practices. Just as he respected the recipients of charity, so he respected the donors. These same attitudes also guided those he deputed to seek the support of others. For this reason, the following section is divided into three: donors; petitioners (or fundraisers); and recipients.

1. Respect Donors

Vincent taught that those approaching donors should in all cases respect them by presenting an honest and simple presentation of needs. The following forms part of his instructions to his fellow priests sent to solicit alms for the poor:

> The distributor of alms should present the condition of the poor truly and simply, without exhorting those who help them to continue or to increase their alms. . . . This happens without anyone talking about it, but it suffices to present the need. Donors love directness [*solidité*] and not discourses. And since they act well in all things, it is good for them if someone writes them about the good that they have seen their donations accomplish, and it is right to put oneself in the place of the poor to show great thanks in a few words. Tell them how many poor we are helping ordinarily, what we give them daily, weekly, or monthly, the order that we observe in the distribution, and what this can amount to weekly. (Guichard, vol. 8, p. 125.)

In other words, fundraisers should respect donors by providing data, stories, and information and by being transparent; moreover, they should motivate donors to give again or otherwise get involved.

Respect for the donors should lead the fundraiser
to rely on the strength of firsthand experience
with the needs of the poor.

The quoted paragraph contains several lessons. First, respect for the donors should lead the fundraiser (or "distributor," since Vincent pictured them as already having distributed alms and now are returning to the same donors) to rely on the strength of firsthand experience

19

with the needs of the poor: "[I]t suffices to present the need." His own experience told him that "donors love directness and not discourse." He wanted his team to thank the donors in the name of the poor, showing that the alms distributors had personal acquaintance and contact with the poor. This would make the presentation more direct. Lastly, he urged good accounting of where the funds went: ". . . what we give them daily, weekly, or monthly."

Although the document lacks a note that claims Vincent as the author, it is difficult to escape the conclusion that it came from him. This set of recommendations continues:

> [Tell them] how many weak Catholics have been strengthened in their faith, how many have been brought back to the right way, and the other results brought about by their temporal help when they are joined to good instructions and the good examples of those who have distributed the alms . . . how many parishes in towns and country; how many poor girls in each parish, the number of children, especially orphans and widows who are being helped or who need help, the number of the sick, if there are any.

His own experience showed that almsgiving should have a spiritual component to it as well, particularly the "good instructions and the good examples of those who have distributed the alms." The distributors of alms were charged with giving both temporal assistance and spiritual help through instructions and especially the good examples of their lives. Vincent was also aware of the plight of young women, who were among the most needy because they were regarded as the weakest of society. He placed them first in the list of other classes of the disadvantaged: children, orphans, widows, and the sick.

> Point out the families without beds or furniture, without clothing or any way to earn a living or to look for work. . . . Recount everything that could lead to compassion; always help those most in need and testify through personal experience their real need, without bringing in someone else's experience, and do not be moved by personal recommendations [i.e., special pleading].

Vincent was more than a benefactor or a channel of funds. In this document, as elsewhere, he wanted to be certain that the impoverished would have a "way to earn a living," to be empowered. For this purpose he was known to have seen to the distribution of tools and seeds for those working the land. His conclusion in this remarkable document was to concentrate on "those most in need." He was engaged in a sort of triage among the poor, probably hoping that neighbors who were at least a little better off would help those in greater need. His own experience also taught him that the demands of clout or special pleading by interested parties should have no place in the care of the poor. In another document he praises this precise case: "This gift should never be forgotten: a poor woman gave away her wardrobe and her shoes and came back in bare feet; when someone told her about this, saying that she would be in greater need to receive than to give, she answered with all simplicity of heart that she had donated her best" (Guichard, vol. 6, p. 22).

In appealing to the Ladies of Charity, Vincent sought to involve them in the service of the sick, both individually and collectively, even reaching outside the close-knit group of noblewomen that constituted their organization. Their rule read:

> Besides the service mentioned above that the ladies will offer to the sick poor, each one of them will contribute to the necessary expenses, and each one will donate according to their devotion and will try, as much as they can, that others contribute, in money, linen, bedding, cloth, preserves, or other items that can help the sick poor. (Guichard, vol. 6, p. 92).

Embedded in this appeal was the concept of "holy rivalry," the mutual encouragement to do good that would spur others to charity. A note in the document cited above attempts to engender this competition:

> The liberality of the butchers of St. Sulpice, Ste. Genevieve, of the place aux Veaux, and of St. Nicolas des Champs, who gave five to six thousand pounds of meat for free. The milliners who generously responded with money, decorations, and the materials of their

profession. . . . We expect the same of the chief overseers of merchandise, those in charge of the crafts, and from other groups. The ardent zeal of the pastors to recommend this work in their exhortations, the preachers in their sermons, the hospitals that have allowed collections, the poor who have given from their own necessities, the rich from their abundance, good clergy who have donated their altar vessels [to devastated churches], and the ladies who have given their holy handiwork and their generous contributions for an assortment of so many needs. (Guichard, vol. 6, p. 76).

Vincent also understood that donors needed recognition. Rather than referring, as we would, to their psychological needs, he couched his approach in terms of respect for them. The noblewomen had everything that they needed and more besides, hence gifts and souvenirs were out of the question. He appealed to a larger scriptural perspective by showing that what they were doing was similar to what had been done in the early Church. He told the Ladies at the Hotel Dieu: "You practice what widows of the primitive Church did, namely, to meet the material needs of the poor as they did, and even the spiritual needs of persons of their own sex, as they did" (Doc. 186, CCD 13b:381). He hoped their commitment would be deepened by realizing how similar they were to the widows of centuries past.

Similarly, Vincent also showed the Ladies respect by joining special events to their meetings. Pierre Coste, Vincent's major biographer of the twentieth century, wrote: "Vincent, in order to give greater solemnity to the meetings, from time to time offered the position of chairman to some ecclesiastical dignitary; the Archbishop of Reims on at least two occasions accepted his invitation" (Coste, v. 2, p. 408). In this way, Vincent was offering them recognition for what they were doing, and doubtless increasing their zeal for the work.

His respect also helped him to handle the case of a hostile benefactor. Brother Louis Robineau, his secretary, reports this occasion:

As we will see there was another act of heroic charity that he often repeated. He greatly displeased a gentleman from Paris, . . . who wanted to alter his will and take back what he had given to the Company. This was quite burdensome. At the same time, this same man uttered atrocious insults against the honor and reputation of Monsieur Vincent. Despite all this, Monsieur Vincent never ceased to pray for him. When the man died, Monsieur Vincent would not omit anything that we owe to a benefactor on his death, namely prayers and suffrages. (Robineau, p. 136.)

By accepting a donation for charitable works, we are entering into a relationship with the donor.

Along the same line, Vincent realized that by accepting a donation for his charitable works, he had entered into a relationship with the donor. The donation involved much more than a financial transaction. Robineau informs us:

Once [Vincent] wrote a letter to a benefactor of the Company in 1655, offering to return the gift he had given since he believed that this benefactor might need it. He begged him to consider what belonged to the Company as his own. He told him: "We will sell on your behalf whatever we have, even the chalices. In this way we will do what the canons require, namely to give to our benefactor in his need what he had given us when he was well-off." Then, continuing his discourse, he added: "What I am telling you is not to seek a compliment, but to see it as it is seen in the sight of God, and as I experience it in the depths of my heart." (Robineau, p. 132.)

It is clear how strongly he felt about this and similar cases. He also respected the wishes of the donors, although he felt that when he received a special donation from Queen Anne of Austria, he was obliged to inform others to enflame their charity. Again, Brother Robineau is the source:

[I]t was mentioned that one day the queen mother gave Monsieur Vincent her earrings to help the poor. . . . When the queen had given her earrings to Monsieur Vincent, she insisted that he not talk to anyone about this, and even repeated this request. Then Monsieur Vincent answered with an exclamation: "Madame, Your Majesty will please pardon me, if I cannot keep hidden such a beautiful act of charity. It is good for all Paris to know of this, Madame, and I will talk about it everywhere." Monsieur Vincent told us this himself. (Robineau, pp. 111–12.)

In other words, the need for charity trumped the need for privacy.

2. Use Disciplined Petitioners

Those who asked for funds were never to be immune from obligations touching their own lives. Vincent knew well enough that access to wealth and power could corrupt even the most devoted person. As a result, he maintained great prudence and reserve in dealing with the rich and powerful, foreswearing any exercise of power through influence.

Vincent maintained his own low profile, avoiding the trappings of power through outward show.

Vincent's practice was to be poor himself. It has been said that one of the great turning points in his life was when he realized that he was poor and consequently powerless (my thanks to Hugh O'Donnell, C.M., for this insight). This was part of his commitment to searching for the presence of God in all he did and in all that happened to him. When he had to look for financial support, he maintained his own low profile, avoiding the trappings of power through outward show. In this way, he anticipated the modern concern about the cost of fundraising by using the funds well and by acknowledging that the resources were to help the poor. Robineau preserved a major excerpt from a conference in which Vincent spoke about the property of the Congregation:

[T]here are two essential truths that must be presupposed: the first is that the temporal property of the Church is something dedicated to God, and that one may not legitimately use it for another purpose than for the service of his divine Majesty; the second is that it is the patrimony of Jesus Christ and of the poor that allows us to benefit by taking only: 1) our food and very moderate support; 2) what is needed to furnish the other costs of the foundation. And when that is done, the rest should be used for the nourishment of the poor, who are the members of the same Jesus Christ. (Robineau, pp. 47–48.)

Writing for the members of the Tuesday Conferences—a voluntary group of clergy devoted to their personal spiritual improvement and the help of others—Vincent urged them to proceed simply during the missions they were called on to give. During the closing procession, for example, he urged them "to avoid grandiosity, too many vestments, ceremonies, and expenses, doing these actions with all necessary simplicity and modesty" (Guichard, vol. 2, p. 15). Put another way, the petitioner was to follow the old adage: Practice what you preach. The petitioner should avoid show, use funds well, avoid useless expenses, and especially give when possible from personal funds, thus offering the good example of charitable giving. This was Vincent's own practice, as Robineau recorded:

Before [Monsieur Vincent's] death, a Master of Requests [a high-level judicial officer of administrative law] asked him to ask the Ladies of Charity for alms for a poor person. He did so but obtained nothing. When he returned from the meeting, he had me called and asked me to find this good gentleman and tell him that he had been unable to obtain anything for the poor man that he had mentioned to him. However, Monsieur Vincent then gave me six écus to give to this good gentleman to distribute them as he judged best. This so edified this Master of Requests that he told me: "This is marvelous. Monsieur Vincent does not only content himself with asking others to provide charity for the poor, but he also gives from his own funds." (Robineau, p. 126).

To concretize the need, Vincent urged that the plight of the poor be portrayed in such a way as to elicit compassion. Then the petitioner would experience their plight in his own heart. As to the first, his "Relations" were carefully written to appeal to the senses of the readers by presenting sights, sounds, smell, even taste, as in the following written about St.-Quentin:

> While another priest was making his rounds, he found many doors closed, but he had them opened and found that the sick were so weak that they could not even open the door, since they had not eaten for three days. They had only half-rotten straw to lie on. The number of these poor folk was so large that, without the help sent from Paris when they expected a siege [of St.-Quentin], the gentlemen of the city, unable to feed them, had decided to throw them over the city walls. . . . In the monastery of the Franciscan Sisters, the need was such that its fifty nuns were reduced to eating bread made of grass and barley, along with some onions. (Feillet, 264–97.)

Vincent shared with his community his deepest feelings about such disasters: "He told us one day that [some]thing bothered him terribly because of the responsibility that he had [as superior general]: . . . that we could not hurry to the aid of the poor as we ought. He said this concerning the two provinces of Champagne and Picardy" (Robineau, p. 136).

All things considered, it could also be said that, for Vincent, fundraising was more than just an occupation; it was a calling. As such, it demanded deep personal commitment and engagement with the range of issues facing the poor.

3. Value Recipients

One of the most illustrative examples of Vincent's respectful approach to the poor is found in a talk he gave to his fellow priests about the duty of evangelizing the poor. Some of them had been ignoring this task, but he held up to them the figure of Jesus speaking simply to the Samaritan woman at the well in Nablus: "Once he was there, Jesus began to instruct that woman by asking for some water. 'Woman, give me some water,' he said to her." On this basis, even the brothers in the farmyard could approach a poor and uninstructed person: "So he [the brother] can ask one, then the other. '*Eh bien!* How are your horses getting along? How's this? How's that? How are you doing?' beginning in this way with something similar and then moving on to our plan [for evangelizing]" (Conf. to CM 161, CCD 11:344). Using these simple words, the brother could approach the poor person with respect, beginning with something that he or she could talk about.

"Whenever [Vincent] would speak to some poor person, it was most often with his hat or his biretta in his hand."

Another example comes from the rules for the Confraternity of Charity at Châtillon—an organization established to serve the poor of the parish—describing with what respect the women members should serve the sick poor:

> [S]he will prepare the dinner and take it to the patients, greeting them cheerfully and kindly. She will set up the tray on the bed, place on it a napkin, a cup, a spoon, and some bread, wash the patient's hands, and then say grace. She will pour the soup into a bowl, and put the meat on a plate. She will arrange everything on the bed tray, then kindly encourage the patient to eat for the love of Jesus and his holy mother. She will do all this as lovingly as if she were serving her own son—or rather God, who considers as done to himself the good she does for persons who are poor.

This document dates from 1617, early in Vincent's life. It shows the thoughtful approach he already had and which formed part of his manner throughout life. Robineau preserved several recollections about this way of acting.

> When some poor peasant from the country came to see him, or some poor prisoner or slave released from captivity, [Vincent] had

them sit down next to him in his room. He used to talk with them with such happiness, goodness, and humility that everyone who saw them was edified by it. This is what I have seen several times. (Robineau, p. 44.)

Another act of respect has to be placed in the hierarchically arranged society of his time, when the type and use of head covering had social significance: "Whenever he would speak to some poor person, it was most often with his hat or his biretta in his hand. He conferred with them and spoke to them at meetings with such meekness and humility that those who saw him were edified by it" (Robineau, p. 42.)

Conclusion

One could cite many other examples of Vincent's seriousness of purpose, focused on the centrality of God's work and respect for every human person.

In an era when fundraising was primarily relegated to beggars begging, Vincent launched fundraising schemes on the grand scale—from the court of France to the simple peasant. And he did it on an international basis. He taught his followers how to treat donors with meticulous instructions. He demanded transparency and, above all, honesty with every donor.

As an empathetic individual, Vincent understood in his own heart the trials of the poor. As a contemplative in action, he took the time needed to reflect deeply on his response. This is what has led him to be called, among other titles, the "Apostle of Charity."

Questions for Discussion

1. Vincent offered detailed instructions on how to treat donors. Name one or two ways our organization is careful and respectful of donors to our mission.

2. What do we do to show respect, provide feedback, and inspire donors?

3. How transparent is our organization in our reporting where the funds are spent? How do we measure the good we do?

4. Vincent offers the concept of "holy rivalry," the mutual encouragement to do good that would spur others to charity. How do we offer holy rivalry in our organization and activities?

3

Revitalizing the Ladies of Charity

Patricia M. Bombard, B.V.M.

[S]ome devout young women and virtuous inhabitants . . .
have decided . . . to assist spiritually and corporally the people
of their town who have sometimes suffered a great deal, more
through a lack of organized assistance than from lack of
charitable persons.

—Vincent de Paul

THE VINCENTIAN STORY of organized charity began nearly 400 years ago. It was Sunday, August 20, 1617. The place was a small French town called Châtillon-les-Dombes. St. Vincent de Paul had recently arrived there to serve as a parish priest. At the time, the town had about 2,000 inhabitants. While some in the town were wealthy aristocrats, conditions for the rural poor surrounding the village were harsh.

On that August Sunday morning, just as he was preparing to say Mass, Vincent had a visitor who would tell him something that would dramatically change the course of his own life and the lives of many others. This is how Vincent himself describes the incident:

> As I was vesting for Mass, a messenger came to tell me that in an
> isolated house about a kilometer from there, everyone was sick, leaving

no one strong enough to care for the others, and that all of them were in indescribable need. This touched me deeply.

Following his sermon during Mass, Vincent encouraged his parishioners to go to the family's aid. What happened next was extraordinary. As he set out that afternoon on foot to visit the family, Vincent met many women from his parish who were coming and going from the house. Again, here is how Vincent describes the scene:

> As it was summertime the heat was great, and these good ladies were stopping along the wayside to rest and refresh themselves. Finally . . . there were so many that it looked like a procession.

After visiting with the family and offering his own comfort to them, Vincent got busy organizing the effort. "I suggested to all these good people whom charity had inspired to visit the sick family that they could tax themselves one day each, to put something into the stew pot, not only for the one family, but for those who would follow," explains Vincent.

Three days later, Vincent brought together seven women from the village to whom he offered a charter for organizing the first "Confraternity of Charity," a sisterhood of charity later known as "The Ladies of Charity." He invited the women to commit to helping the needy out of their own resources, each on her allotted day.

Lessons in the Story

What lessons for a sustainable approach to charity can we draw from this Vincentian story? First, it is significant to note that Vincent did not simply invite his parishioners to take up a special collection of funds at the Mass to pay for food that someone else would prepare and deliver to the sick family in order to help them. Instead, he invited them to give regularly of their own time, talent, and food resources. Vincent apparently knew that money, after all, could come from a number of sources, but without the involvement of good people, there would be little meaning or value and consequently little success and sustainability in the work.

Our first lesson, then, is that a successful charitable effort starts with tapping the goodness in people. For Vincent, creating the Confraternities of Charity was not just about the charity, it was also about forming and strengthening community. Vincent once said, "What a benefit to be in a community where [every] single person participates in the good done by all its members."

A successful charitable effort starts with tapping the goodness in people.

Secondly, Vincent recognized that the charitable effort at Châtillon needed leadership. The effort needed someone to come forward with vision, organizational skills, and an effective management style. Vincent had all of these, and he put them to work. As a recent biography written by Bernard Pujo tells us:

> From the beginning of his apostolate, Vincent de Paul was a man of action, an organizer and manager. He did not throw himself into a venture in haphazard fashion. Rather, he decided on a program, defined a method, and made sure of acquiring the wherewithal for the project. (Pujo, p. 71.)

We can see Pujo's description of Vincent evident in his approach and actions at Châtillon. Vincent had a vision for the charitable work there—a plan for how to sustain and broaden the charity beyond that Sunday afternoon. Key to Vincent's ideal for the women he would draw into that vision was serving directly with people in need, providing them both material and spiritual enrichment. However, Vincent's vision went beyond the needs of those served. A critical element of his vision was the reasoning that such charity would not benefit only those who received soup and bread. Vincent's approach made the benefits go both ways. He insisted that the women also work at "cultivating humility, simplicity, and charity in themselves" (Pujo, p. 65). In other words, at the heart of

Vincentian service is the recognition that tied to one's service is one's own personal or spiritual development. This insight provided a dual, deeply personal, and spiritual motivation for the long-term commitment of the members of a Confraternity.

Tied to one's service is one's own personal or spiritual development.

Vincent also had the organizational skill to make the effort sustainable—in other words, an awareness of how to give the effort a structure to ensure it existed over time. How he gained this managerial skill is unknown, but his effective, innovative management style enabled him to enlist the women of the town to make a commitment to carry out the vision.

As Pujo tells us, by December of that same year (1617), Vincent completed a detailed written "rule" for the Confraternity. On December 8, the bishop of Lyon gave Vincent the decree recognizing the new Confraternity of Charity and its regulations, and this document was placed in the chapel of Châtillon for safekeeping (Pujo, p. 65–66).

The Model Spreads

Shortly thereafter, Vincent left Châtillon-les-Dombes for another assignment. However, he carried with him the plan he had created at Châtillon for establishing more Confraternities with him: visiting a locale, preaching there a mission of forgiveness and reconciliation, then creating a Confraternity of Charity to continue the development of local community (Padberg/Hannefin, p. 107).

In 1625, Vincent received funds from his new employers, the de Gondi family, to establish the Congregation of the Mission, a formal community of fellow priests who would help expand Vincent's vision. The founding of the congregation meant more priests, more missions, and more charities. Eventually, the Confraternities extended throughout France, with hundreds of women forming communities committed to meeting the needs of people living in poverty while attending to their own spiritual growth.

While Vincent instructed the women who formed the first Confraternity to meet the needs of the poor from their own wealth, the need for additional funds to sustain the effort soon became evident. Vincent's leadership had provided both a community of people with hands and hearts ready and willing to do the work and the organizational structure to keep them together and properly directed. These efforts gained the credibility and respect the Confraternities needed to begin raising the funds to meet their goal of being "servants to the poor."

Leadership Extends to Louise

By 1625, the Confraternities had grown so numerous and had been operating so long without direct supervision that Vincent became concerned about their viability. He quickly found an answer to his concern in the very capable management skills of a Parisian aristocrat, Louise de Marillac (later sainted for her work, as he was). Vincent charged Louise with traveling to the remote villages to oversee the management of the charities. As Padberg and Hannefin tell us:

> [Louise] instructed and inspired the ladies, recruited and trained new members, taught the children, visited the poor in their homes, nursed the sick, trained schoolmistresses, and gave the example of all that a servant of the poor should be. Through these visits she completed the work of organization that Vincent had begun. (Padberg and Hannefin, p. 108.)

In 1630, Louise began a Confraternity in her own parish, Saint Nicholas-du-Chardonnet, which she also led. Within a short time, nearly every parish in Paris and the surrounding countryside had its own Confraternity. The members of these organizations were mostly women from the aristocracy, who were not accustomed to cooking and serving and also soon felt the burden of service was infringing on their time to manage their own household. Louise and Vincent responded by creating the Daughters of Charity, a congregation of religious women whose membership was drawn mostly from the peasant class. This relationship between the Daughters and the Ladies proved to be a bond that has carried over the centuries, with the Daughters eventually not only providing direct service to the poor, but also with many Daughters providing ongoing spiritual formation to the Confraternities in their role as spiritual moderators.

From the Past to Today

What of the Confraternities of Charity today? To answer that, we will look in on the operations of the organization, more popularly known today as the Ladies of Charity in the United States, as they prepare in 2017 to mark their founding's four-hundredth anniversary.

Interestingly, Vincent's early model of bringing together a group of women eager to be of help, offering them the dual motivations of service and spiritual growth, and encouraging innovative responses to the needs of the poor still applies to these efforts.

Today, the worldwide family of what once was known as the Confraternities of Charity is called the Association of International Charities (AIC). The AIC present structure includes associations and local chapters—53 associations worldwide, in Africa, Latin America, Asia, Europe, and in the United States, where there are chapters in 22 states. Individual members (all women) presently number some 150,000. Among these, about 20,000 are in a position of leadership. The 400-year anniversary will be a time of renewal and of new departure for the coming years. For the remainder of this chapter, we will briefly examine these revitalization efforts, beginning with the worldwide effort of the AIC, and then using as examples the national and local groups in the United States.

The AIC reported in 2013 that more than 13,800 projects around the world are dedicated to fighting poverty. To provide support for these efforts, the AIC's operational guidelines for 2011–2015 focus on education, seen as a two-way process:

1. To identify and value skills and potential
2. To encourage interdependence
3. To promote co-creativity.

Today's members of the AIC are keenly aware of their commitment to the core values and legacy of Vincent de Paul and Louise de Marillac. Yet, they also are prepared to embark in new directions, meeting the needs of a new century.

For examples of how the AIC is undergoing revitalization focused on growing membership and assuring financial stability, we turn now to the story of the national association in the United States and some of its individual association members.

AIC in the United States

It was a young woman named Catherine Harkins who founded the first Ladies of Charity in the United States. In 1857 at the age of 23, Harkins moved with her steamboat-captain husband to St. Vincent de Paul Parish in St. Louis. There, encouraged by the Vincentian priests who staffed the parish, she and 11 other women officially formed the association, with Harkins acting as the first president, and began to visit the poor and elderly in the area. According to historians:

> The Panic of 1857, caused by unsound banks and depressed prices for farm products, caused a depression that was to continue until the outbreak of the Civil War. There were many hungry poor in St. Louis, and the new association found its services to be much in demand. In order to raise funds, the Ladies asked the Strackosh Opera Troupe to give a benefit matinee performance, the first of its kind in St. Louis, at Mercantile Hall. (Padberg/Hannefin, p. 111.)

Soon, word of the St. Louis group spread, and other associations formed. Nearly 100 years later, the number of women volunteering as Ladies of Charity in the United States had reached 40,000. The idea emerged to create a national organization, and the Ladies of Charity USA (LCUSA) officially formed in 1960.

The number of members in the all-volunteer organization declined severely following the 1960s, "when women went to work," said Gayle Johnson, who served as national president in 2012–2013. (Johnson and I corresponded via email to discuss LCUSA.) The organization now numbers about 8,000 women serving through 68 local associations in 21 states. It is undergoing revitalization after adopting a five-year action plan in the spring of 2013. Goals of the plan include:

- Increase membership through personal invitation and strategic use of social media.
- Develop a process that will deepen spirituality for members.
- Engage the national board and membership in advocacy, especially on behalf of women and children living in poverty.
- Grow and diversify funding for the Ladies of Charity nationally and locally, and sustain fiscal responsibility.
- Increase communication and visibility of the Ladies of Charity locally, nationally, and internationally.

With the revitalization effort in mind, the LCUSA also recently adopted a Mission and Vision Statement as follows:

Mission Statement

To provide Vincentian leadership to women acting together against all forms of poverty.

Vision Statement

LCUSA-AIC provides Vincentian leadership of transformation [empowering leadership that transforms lives], assisting persons who are vulnerable to move from marginalization and despair to participation and hope.

1. Assist local associations to continue, expand and improve their charitable and spiritual works according to the directives and in the spirit of St. Vincent [de Paul], St. Louise de Marillac, and St. Elizabeth Ann Seton [founder of Sisters of Charity in the United States] through personal service to those in need.

2. Adopt the Vincentian model of systemic change in implementing projects and encourage collaboration with other members of the Vincentian family and comparable organizations in developing the projects.

3. Advocate the rights of those living in poverty.

4. Encourage and aid in communication to promote and strengthen unity, to share ideas and information among all the associations, and to foster the formation of new associations of Ladies of Charity in collaboration with the other branches of the Vincentian family.

5. Foster more vital links with the International Association of Charities (AIC) to profit from the experiences of Ladies of Charity worldwide and to be supportive of sister associations in their efforts to respond to unmet needs.

New Focus on Systemic Change

As LCUSA vision statement indicates, one aspect of the revitalization effort is a focus on systemic change. "Today the work of our association is not only to feed, clothe, and give shelter to those living in poverty but to change situations which degrade the individual and prevent him/her from living their lives with dignity," said Johnson in a message to the membership in the Winter-Spring 2013 issue of the association's newsletter, *Servicette* (p. 3). "The purpose of a national association is to provide training to local associations and to collaborate with other Catholic and nonprofit organizations in implementing projects that break the cycle of poverty and move the individual to personal dignity and control of his/her destiny. In collaborating with these same organizations LCUSA can influence legislation that recognizes the roots of poverty and gives the poor a voice."

Fundraising Done Locally

Local associations operate independently and generally raise funds for services through a variety of local activities including:

- Donations, gifts, and memorials
- Bake sales
- Rummage sales
- Fashion shows and luncheons
- Golf tournaments
- Dinner cruises
- Chili suppers
- Plant sales
- House or church tours
- Auctions
- Thrift stores
- Raffles
- Barbecues
- Collections or bingo at meetings

—*LCUSA Membership Brochure*

In 2011, the AIC published a training booklet entitled, *Fundraising: An Essential Element in the Development of Our Associations.* The introduction to the booklet tells the story of Vincent de Paul's own efforts to raise funds as background to the AIC's own commitment to the work:

It is said that once when Vincent saw the Queen of France, Anne of Austria, adorned with a magnificent river of diamonds, he said to her: "Your Majesty, let these stones be turned to bread." The Queen immediately undid her necklace in order to give it to him.

Throughout his life, Vincent had to act to find financial means. He searched at every level of the network he had built. This included people from the royal court, of course, but also the Ladies of Charity and all his acquaintances. To increase the awareness of his donors, he sent a regular letter, which he called *Relation*.

Fundraising remains an essential element in the life of our AIC associations, quite simply because it allows us to bring to fruition our projects with the poorest and so to accomplish our mission today.

Membership Drive Tied to Service

Re-revitalization plans for the Ladies of Charity USA center on recruitment tied to service opportunities. Expectations of membership in the LCUSA as spelled out in their recruitment brochure include:

- Praying together with and for those served
- Participating in the Eucharist whenever possible
- Studying the lives and teachings of the Vincentian founders
- Attending renewal days and retreats
- Working with Vincentian collaborators and other organizations
- Serving in leadership roles for LCUSA and in the community
- Advocating for just policies and programs
- Attending Vincentian gatherings and LCUSA national assemblies
- Serving in leadership roles for AIC

What follows are some examples of how individual associations in the LCUSA have begun this revitalization effort.

Ladies of Charity of Metropolitan Kansas City

For Gayle Johnson, the Ladies of Charity seemed like a natural fit when she sought to become involved in faith-based volunteer work. Johnson eventually served as president of the Ladies of Charity of

Metropolitan Kansas City in 2006–2007 and at the same time on the national board as regional representative. As mentioned above, she was president of the national board in 2012–2013. She also has served as a representative on AIC's executive board.

Johnson explained that revitalization of the Kansas City association began with a move to focus educational efforts on a renewed understanding of poverty and an attempt to address the issue of violence against women.

In 2006 Allison Boisvert, a social justice minister, spoke to the Ladies of Charity at their annual assembly about the difference between situational and generational poverty. She herself was born into poverty on a Native American reservation. "Her talk was the beginning of a realization that the organization's approach to poverty had been directed only toward meeting immediate needs," commented Johnson in our emails. The LCUSA began to educate the membership about the two types of poverty and the need for a different approach to end generational poverty. A workshop on poverty in Kansas City held later in 2006 was the first of several directed at this goal.

Conference events helped to renew interest and increase involvement. In 2007 a group from the United States attended the AIC international assembly in Rome. The theme was "Violence Directed Against Women." Upon their return from Rome, the group began to look at human trafficking in the United States. That year, Kansas City held another conference focused on women and domestic violence including talks on human trafficking. "Back in 2007, no one in Kansas City was even talking about human trafficking," Johnson states.

Johnson said these conference events, focused on addressing poverty in new ways and on assisting marginalized women in today's society, helped to renew interest and increase involvement in the Ladies of Charity of Metropolitan Kansas City.

New Orleans Revitalization Story

The New Orleans Ladies of Charity is another example of a revitalization effort tied to service. The association joined a coalition of Catholic partners on a direct service project in response to the Katrina disaster. The resulting St. Joseph's Rebuild Center in downtown New Orleans provides services to needy and displaced persons. The New Orleans LC group worked with national leadership to develop a five-point revitalization plan, according to Adrian Kappesser, one of the core members of the association, whom I spoke with in May of 2013. "We are struggling," Kappesser admitted at the time of the group's attempt to implement the plan. "After Katrina many people moved away, and even the people who came back have little time to dedicate to volunteering."

The five-step plan, which was highlighted in the LCUSA Fall 2012 national newsletter, is:

1. Target projects for the poor, systemic change and director service
2. Identify a process to meet needs of the poor
3. Work for "good timing" in the association
4. Vital role of spiritual moderator/spiritual animator
5. Recruitment in the parishes, city or towns for new members

Pre-Katrina, the association had a steady group of core members and hosted two successful annual fundraisers. "For the first year after Katrina, it was pretty much impossible to get donations from companies who were struggling themselves," observed Kappesser. "Now, the city is doing well, but we don't have members."

However, while still lacking in membership, the association did make a commitment to engage in a newly identified service project (step one in the revitalization plan), the collaboration with the St. Joseph's Rebuild Center. The association proposed a monthly birthday party of homeless people, organized and staffed by its members.

"The party was so well received," commented Kappesser on the response of the Center's clients. "It was such an incredible experience. No one had ever said 'happy birthday' to them before. All of a sudden, they were individuals, not just homeless people."

"All of a sudden, they were individuals, not just homeless people."

The association now also provides cake and beverages, and hopes eventually to be able to provide simple birthday gifts, such as a clean pair of socks, to the homeless clients at the Center. More Stories of Revitalization

In 2012, the St. Jerome Ladies of Charity Association in Hyattsville, Maryland, was preparing to celebrate its eightieth anniversary. However, at the start of the year, the impending anniversary might have generated little enthusiasm, as membership had dwindled to only a few women in recent years. That was before Kendra Jochum joined the parish. Jochum already had a strong history of active service with the Ladies of Charity in another parish. When she moved into St. Jerome Parish and asked if there was an active association present, the pastor looked at her and candidly said, "You're it!" He then provided her with names and phone numbers of inactive previous members as well as Therese Mukoko, who was the only other member he knew of who was actively interested in recharging the ministry. In the end, the eightieth anniversary of the association turned out to be a remarkable story of revitalization that is both inspiring and informative.

Together, Jochum and Mukoko (serving as president and vice president respectively) worked steadily over the next several months to successfully revive the association, adding 14 new members by August 2012. They also worked to establish a Junior Ladies of Charity, starting with a few interested girls and tripling membership within a few short months.

A major factor in the revitalization effort was the support of the pastor of St. Jerome, Fr. James Stack, and Beverly Motley and Gloria Rose of the Archdiocese of Washington Ladies of Charity. Jochum said, "We had one meeting in April 2012 to discuss revitalizing the Ladies of Charity group, and then I took it from there. The work began in earnest in the spring of 2012 with a 'Taste and See Information Meeting.' The emphasis on no commitments beyond doing 'what you can when you can' helped to open the door for women to get involved. There was and still is a hesitancy from others about over-committing themselves with other family and professional responsibilities to balance."

"The emphasis on no commitments beyond doing 'what you can when you can' helped to open the door for women to get involved."

Capitalizing on the renewed interest, the leadership scheduled monthly meetings, continuing to focus on growing membership through publicity initiatives. The members created a presentation board permanently placed in the vestibule of the church to provide background and current information on the Ladies of Charity. They created flyers to place in weekly church bulletins, a Facebook page (www.facebook.com/StJeromesLadiesofCharity), an email address, and a business card with mission and contact information.

The growth in membership allowed the association to create new service committees and extend its service work within both the parish and the local community. These service activities include an impressive list, with some already established and some still pending: monthly material donation drives; helping the sick, elderly, and needy with chores, errands, transportation, and companionship; arranging clothing exchanges and a clothes closet; supporting victims of domestic violence through the local Family Crisis Center; providing meals to individuals and families in difficulty; supporting a maternity home and a local pregnancy center; supporting local nursing homes through social visits and group activities; supporting the student center at a local university; supporting prison outreach; and connecting with the Nigerian community at St. Jerome's to enjoy cross-cultural relationships and identify a sister parish community.

Re-Founded Ladies of Charity in Indianapolis

Mary Nell Williams tells the story of the re-founding of The Ladies of Charity of Indianapolis in the Fall 2012 issue of *Servicette*. According to Williams, the Indianapolis association began with four members in 1945 and continued until the 1980s, when the group formally disbanded due to declining membership.

After no activity for some 30 years, in the spring of 2011 two Indianapolis women, Valerie Roraus and Val Kappes, were looking for a way to serve. They asked Sr. Sharon Richardt, Daughter of Charity, for advice. She directed them to Jude Magers, a Daughter of Charity affiliate in Indianapolis, who asked Mary Nell Williams, also an affiliate, to join her in helping the women to explore the idea of reviving the local association of the Ladies of Charity USA. They also spread the word to other women "known to have good Vincentian hearts."

The group, now grown to eight in size, gathered in January 2012 to hear more about the Ladies of Charity and their own sense of a call to service. The participants received questions to consider in advance and an invitation to attend a retreat in April, where further discussion occurred. Magers and Williams prepared the contents of the retreat and invited Sr. Fran Ryan, Daughter of Charity and LCUSA spiritual moderator, to be a presenter. Everyone on the retreat agreed to continue to work on creating a formal association. By the close of the retreat, the group had elected its first officers and a spiritual moderator. Their further work included applying for a charter, appealing for seed money, establishing bank accounts, writing articles of incorporation, obtaining a tax identification number, and writing the bylaws.

Fundraising is first of all about "friend-raising."

The re-founded association held its first formal meeting in June, and meetings have occurred monthly since. The officers were installed and 17 women were celebrated as charter members at a Mass on September 22. "During the course of all of their work in the past 15 months, the members have been and continue to be deliberate in their remembrance of the Ladies of Charity of Indianapolis who preceded them," wrote Williams.

The story of the Ladies of Charity of Indianapolis illustrates once again the first lesson in fundraising—that it begins with tapping into the goodness of people and maintaining the human bonds that result from establishing relationships. Fundraising is first of all about "friend-raising."

Ladies of Charity Diocese of Buffalo

In 1941, the women volunteers in eight counties of the Diocese of Buffalo formed a local unit of Ladies of Charity patterned after the existing groups in St. Louis and several other cities across the United States. The intent was to coordinate efforts, increase communication, pool resources, and better serve the poor. The initial ceremony saw 2,000 women enrolled; by 1962, enrollment peaked at 16,000, with hundreds of thousands of individuals and families assisted through Ladies of Charity projects over the years.

As with other associations through the United States, one of the biggest challenges facing the Buffalo association is to boost membership, which had dropped to under 1,400 in 2013. Leadership has also identified the need to expand Junior Units, and to promote racial diversity and understanding within the membership. In addition, the association hopes to become more effective advocates for social change. Membership is open to women of all faiths and ages.

Conclusion

Vincent de Paul's first organized response to the impoverished occurred nearly 400 years ago, when he saw charity present in the hearts of women responding with food to a needy family at Châtillon. He soon gathered the women together with a plan for a sustained charitable response, which he supplemented with a plan to provide ongoing financial resources. The examples of revitalization with the Ladies of Charity USA give witness to this trinity of factors needed to sustain an effective response to the poor still in operation today: openness to inspiration moving in the hearts of individuals; the support of others able to ignite that call into action within a formal, collaborative structure; and the financial resources to turn ideas into active service.

Questions for Discussion

1. How does our organization see and seek the goodness in others willing to provide assistance to those in need, especially the poor?

2. Who inspires us to action? In what ways do we inspire others?

3. What strategies do we need to put in place to ensure the long-term viability of our organization?

4

Sustaining Operations through Major and Planned Gifts

Mark Pranaitis, C.M.

*The day will come when the Company will have greater
credibility and support, and those who can do good for it will
have greater charity for it than they do now.*
—Vincent de Paul

DEVELOPMENT DIRECTORS and other executives within nonprofit organizations often dream of a day when they will not have to worry about raising money because there will be enough of it to sustain the organization. I know this because I am one of them. I have spoken with enough others to conclude that this dream is not mine alone. It is widely shared by pastors, presidents, and other leaders, who can grow weary from having to ask for funds to fuel their organizations. For the dream-filled leader, the longed-for gift is the multi-million dollar check that will fully fund an endowment allowing all other fundraising activities to cease.

As long as there is work to do, we must raise money.

We know that day will never come. It is the nature of the mission of nonprofit organizations never to end. Few are the nonprofits whose missions (markets) go away like the often-referenced buggy whip or typewriter factory. Rather, education, job training, food, clothing, shelter, health care, and all the other services nonprofits provide will always be needed somewhere by someone. I suspect there always will be someone left on the margins of society or outside of the system, no matter how much progress we make. Until no one is in need, our organizations will have plenty to do. As long as there is work to do, we must raise money.

Thinking Big from the Beginning

Many organizations begin their development efforts by making an appeal to friends, family members, colleagues, and anyone else with a connection to the organization. This happens at an event, through a written solicitation, or both. Many times the event or request becomes an annual tradition. We hire staff to manage these things because they are the cornerstone of our organization's annual funding. For parishes, the weekly collection typically provides the base of operational funding. This may be augmented by a Lenten fish fry, a youth-group picnic, or more.

Over time, these activities, if well-managed, become more valuable since through them we learn the giving patterns and interests of our donors. However, these annual activities can grow tiresome. It may be in the middle of re-writing the brochure for the umpteenth time or ensuring the website includes the proper information for this year's appeal that it dawns on you (like it dawns on me) that a really big check would make life so much easier not merely for me but for the whole organization. Isn't there someone who will write us that check so we can get on with the mission rather than having to raise money?

We Need to Ask

More than likely your organization already knows many people who can write larger checks. Maybe you have been asking them to increase their gift each year or you have started a giving society for those who give $1,000, $5,000 or more. But getting around to asking for those larger gifts seems impossible, what with the photos due to the printer and the annual report data due to the CFO, and someone has to find eleven more silent auction items before Friday. Who has time to ask for the big money? Why doesn't someone realize we do great work here and send us a check with many zeroes?

If we are not asking for major gifts, we are also missing the opportunity to invite our donors more deeply into their own spiritual path.

Those checks arrive in the movies. Motivational speakers tell stories about them. But rarely is an organization surprised by a large check some donor just happened to send. Rather, donors make major gifts because someone has asked them for it. If we are not asking our donors for major gifts, why not? If we are not organized to do this then we must reorganize—because if we are not asking them then we are not inviting our donors to commit more deeply to the mission of our organization. It is not merely the money our organizations are missing if we are not asking for major gifts. We are also missing the opportunity to invite our donors more deeply into their own spiritual path.

To ask for major and planned gifts we must have a story to tell, one that is big enough to warrant asking for a sizeable gift. We also must have organizational support. This is why we must think big. If our organization fulfills a mission that is large enough and serves enough people in substantial ways, we will be able to ask for and receive large gifts. Asking for and receiving major and planned gifts are not done in the spare time of an already overly committed development office. We must plan for and staff these vitally important positions. If we don't do these things, we may hear about our donor's gifts being made to other organizations—ours is not the only good work out there.

Take the Long View

Few are the nonprofit organizations that begin with a fully staffed development office capable of coordinating day-to-day operations along with the annual appeal, an event or two, and asking for and receiving major and planned gifts. However, in the same way that parents must anticipate that their children will not always be babies or toddlers, the wise organization anticipates and plans for growth in the development office until all aspects of development including major gifts and planned giving are appropriately (proportionately) staffed and funded. This demands taking the long view on things, which, from my perspective, is the foundation for being able to think big about mission and the revenues needed to sustain that mission.

Even the huge organizations started small. Within them was a big vision.

Most organizations start small but have a big dream. But the organization doesn't start with the cure for cancer. Rather, even the huge research hospitals from which a cure may come started small. Within them was a big vision. Those who organized well found donors, cultivated those donors, and reaped the rewards of growth. Certainly not all of this growth happened in a straight-line trajectory. Most organizations had to take a leap at various points. They took a chance, hopefully a very calculated one, and grew as a result. The same is true for the development offices that help provide essential funding. At some point organizational leaders assigned staff to focus on asking for and receiving major and planned gifts. Without that foresight they would have been less likely to tap into the accumulated wealth of their donors (from which most major gifts come) or to receive a portion of their donors' estates (from which bequests or legacy gifts come).

While Stephen Covey gets the credit for listing "begin with the end in mind" as one of the seven habits of highly effective people, this bit of wisdom long predates him. For the fundraising organization, beginning with the end in mind includes organizing to ask for major and planned gifts even before your organization is ready to do this. If you don't plan for this, it is very hard to get there. The "tyranny of the present" (again, Stephen Covey) takes over, and you could find yourself busy with the annual appeal and the St. Patrick's Day Auction. You never get around to asking for larger amounts and more complicated gifts.

I know of which I write very personally. In the early 1990s, I founded a housing organization in Denver, Colorado: Annunciation Housing Partners (later, Neighborhood Partners). I was a seminary intern in a parish when I started Partners. There was this boarded-up house across the street from the parish church. I wanted us to buy it, renovate it, and sell it to a working poor family. We did exactly that. Then we did it again and again and again.

At the start we incorporated, formed a board, raised money, hired staff. Several of us worked endless hours. It all was worth it. But, if I had dedicated resources to seeking larger sums and legacy gifts, working poor families might still be moving into homes built or renovated by Neighborhood Partners. They aren't. After a good run, the organization lost ground to other, better funded housing providers. There simply never seemed to be the time to deepen our donor relationships and prepare to ask for those major gifts. There never seemed to be enough money to hire a person to focus solely on this work. In the end, another housing organization, one with an international reputation, had the resources to buy vacant lots and distressed houses even as the prices of these increased. We were not able to keep up.

We had a good run. Over 15 years we built and renovated an impressive number of homes. Some of them had custom features designed to accommodate children and adults with special needs. Our families connected deeply to our organization and the community. Many parishes and businesses supported us with donations (money and in-kind) and countless volunteers hammered, painted, and shingled until the house was finished. We did so many things right. Neighborhood Partners could still be doing this work if we had asked for and received major and legacy gifts.

We did so many things right. We could still be doing this work if we had asked for and received major and legacy gifts.

We began with one end in mind: renewing families and communities through home ownership. But, we missed another end that is very necessary. Major and planned gifts are the end result of mature donor relationships. Donors make the commitment of major and planned gifts because they have a mature relationship with the organization. The wise organization begins with the end in mind. That end includes major and planned gifts. This isn't about greed. It is about getting to know your donor so well and allowing your donor to know you and your organization so well that the gift is natural, not at all forced, even though you still have to ask for it.

Let me encourage you to begin with this end in mind: every donor will become a major donor and will leave a planned gift. Even if your organization has been around for a long time and even if your development effort has been hosting its annual event for decades, you can still begin anew. Vincent de Paul's switch to his life work came during his middle age. So, too, can our conversion and that of our organization as well. Doing this will allow your organization to sustain its operations into the future thanks to an increasing stream of funding from multiple sources.

A Stewardship Approach

If you ask average Catholics what stewardship means, they might say it has to do with sharing one's "time, talent, and treasure" with their parish. They've heard this from the pulpit for many years, but in my view it is an elementary and insufficient understanding of stewardship. It focuses on the object of the stewardship—the parish—instead of on the steward. It serves the parish's purpose (which is why it has taken hold in the minds of pastors, most of whom enjoy fundraising about as much as dental surgery). A more comprehensive and nuanced understanding is rarely taught from the pulpit, in the parish classroom, or in the diocesan newspaper.

To expand on this definition, stewards in the Catholic tradition understand that all we are and have is a gift from God and God asks us to be generous with these gifts. We express this generosity (or not) within our household, to family members, at our parish, on the job, in our neighborhoods, and within the larger society. It does not matter if we receive compensation for what we do, if we volunteer, or if the object of our generosity is our spouse or child. We are stewards if we acknowledge God's gift, thank him for those gifts, share those gifts generously and responsibly, and are willing to be held accountable for them.

The typical "stewardship report" in a parish bulletin, however, includes things like last week's offertory collection, how much the collection was last year at the same time, and how much is needed to operate the parish. There may be other collections listed as well (building fund or the like). For a really progressive parish, there might be an item noting the number of service hours people gave to the parish that week. This method of reporting reinforces the "time, talent, treasure" approach to stewardship.

It is a fine report in that it shows transparency and accountability, but what about other forms of service? What about the parishioners who care for elderly parents or a handicapped child at home and who don't serve on parish committees because of these commitments? Are they not providing a valuable service, a recognizable ministry? Are they not being good stewards? Similarly, what of the business leaders who coach Little League sports after work? Is this not a sharing of their talents?

Generosity begets generosity.

Generosity begets generosity. When was the last time you heard a fundraiser encourage his donors to be generous to other organizations, such as the college they attended? Rather, I suspect most fundraisers (privately) gripe when they hear about gifts to other places. While I know every organization needs support of all kinds, this shallow understanding of stewardship as focused on only one's own "team" does nothing to get us what we need. With our elementary and insufficient understanding of stewardship focused solely on ourselves, we are not taking into account the larger universe in which the steward (donor) lives.

Development directors who are rooted in stewardship understand that what needs to be activated is the generosity of the donor's decision-making process on every level. Fundraisers sometimes claim they are competing for the same charitable dollars. While this makes sense since even the wealthiest person has a last dollar and a million dollar gift to one charity means that the same million dollars cannot be given to my organization, there is a factor that is missing in this line of thinking. Not every donor is attracted to every cause.

Ask yourself why you don't give to every charitable organization that solicits from you. I suggest the answer is more about how much you care for the causes they represent and not merely because you don't have a limitless source of funds to give away. The reason you care about certain charities is because something in your heart calls you to them. If we all wanted to support nothing other than organizations that provide food to poor people, we would have a lot of well-fed homeless, naked, and uneducated people walking around.

Instead, what we have are multiple organizations that respond to a variety of needs. We support those organizations that serve the causes and people we care about. We are moved from within to care about some more than others. This prompts us to be generous to the organizations that respond to the things we care about. We give to them and not to others. This is how it should be.

We are moved from within to care about some causes more than others.

Returning to my own story, I started a housing organization. There were many other services the people of Annunciation Parish needed. But I know housing. I notice housing. I care about housing. I do not know health care, literacy, or domestic abuse. Surely programs offering every one of these things (and more) could have operated in the Annunciation neighborhood. However, I was not the one to start them because these are not the things to which I have the capacity to respond. In my personal life, I have been a successful real estate broker and developer. I believe God helped me to be successful in that endeavor. Through Partners, I put those gifts to work in a new and different way. Housing is my thing. Hence, my time, talent, and treasure disproportionately supported Annunciation Housing Partners because I experienced the call from within asking me to do this.

Faith-filled fundraisers see themselves as partners with donors. Instead of sitting across the table from each other, the two sit together across the table from the Divine. At that table, they will together discern the right choices for the donor. The fundraiser, based on the strength of the established relationship, is able to advise the donor as to how his or her money can help the organization. Faith-filled donors are similarly alert to discerning if they feel a call in the direction of the organization's request.

Mature Donor Relationships

Most donor relationships do not begin with a request for a major gift. Even if a donor's first gift to your organization is large by your organization's standards, the relationship with the donor must be developed. Like any relationship, this happens through a series of meetings, conversations, visits, and other engagements. Over time, the donor will get to know your organization and appreciate its mission and approach to fulfilling that mission. The donor's continued interest, expressed through regular giving, serving on committees or the board, or other ways, will show how much he or she likes and respects the organization and what it does. In short, all donors, by virtue of the fact that they give to our organizations at all, know us, like us, know what we do, and like what we do. If they didn't, they wouldn't give. If that is the case for the average donor, it is only more so for the mature donors who must really know us, like us, know what we do, and like what we do if they are going to give major and planned gifts to our organization.

No one can be expected to give a large sum to an organization they do not know well.

Continuing this theme of relationships, major donors and those who give planned gifts show their commitment to our organizations through these gifts. Looked at a different way, no one could reasonably be expected to give a large sum to an organization they did not know well and respect or whose work they did not appreciate. This, then, is the goal of everyone with fundraising responsibility—to cultivate mature donor relationships. Without these relationships, the organization will not be able to ask for major and planned gifts.

Defining Major and Planned Gifts

Each organization determines the amount of its major gifts. The amount varies from organization to organization based, especially, on the size of the organization. A university or hospital with an annual budget of several hundred million dollars and which raises tens of millions of dollars through charitable gifts each year will probably define major gifts at a much higher level than will a local service agency run solely by volunteers with an annual budget of $20,000. To the former, a major gift might be $10,000 or more. To the latter, a $1,000 gift would be major.

Defining a major gift is important. While most fundraisers will agree that every gift is important, given the limited time and resources the fundraiser has, priorities must be set. If every gift is acknowledged with merely the same form letter, the organization is not recognizing the significance of the larger gifts it receives. That recognition is important because it is a part of the cultivation of the relationship that will lead to similarly sized gifts each year or other larger gifts, which come primarily because of a well-developed relationship.

The smart fundraiser is always on the lookout to match donor interests with organizational needs.

Major gifts come for a reason that typically extends beyond the normal operating budget of the organization. Sometimes they happen to help pay for a special need. The smart fundraiser is always on the lookout to match donor interests with organizational needs. Depending upon the size of your organization, everything from a new computer for a key staff member to a major building project is a potential opportunity for you to ask donors for a gift if you have cultivated the relationship to a point where asking for it is appropriate.

Planned Gifts

Major gifts usually come from a donor's earned or investment income. Planned gifts typically come from a donor's accumulated wealth. While some planned gifts are complex, requiring the participation of lawyers and tax accountants, most are rather straightforward. Smart fundraisers know this and are ready to refer donors to skilled professionals when the gift planning grows more complicated than the fundraiser can manage. The wise organization has access to advisors who are willing to lend their expertise to ensure the gift is structured in such a way that the organization and the donor are happy with the final agreement.

Annuities

Annuities are a popular form of planned gift. An annuity is a contract between a donor and the organization. The donor (annuitant) gives an amount of money to the organization in exchange for a regular payment from the organization. The amount the organization will pay is guided by a formula that takes into consideration the age of the annuitant and his or her life expectancy. In short, younger annuitants are paid a lower interest rate over more years and older annuitants are paid a higher interest rate over fewer years. If everything works as it is supposed to, the organization will invest the annuitant's money at an interest rate higher than the amount of interest that will be paid. Upon the death of the annuitant, the payments cease. The organization is then free to use the money given by the annuitant for the purposes stated in the annuity contract.

Many donors are interested in a secure investment that pays a reliable amount.

Annuities are a fairly easy way for an organization and a less-experienced fundraiser to break into the world of planned gifts. Many donors, even those of more moderate means, are interested in a secure investment that pays a reliable and predictable amount. Even small organizations can get involved in selling annuities, though state laws govern the sale of these contracts. Make sure your organization is operating in accord with these laws before advertising to your supporters that you offer annuities.

Through the interactions with donors who want to purchase annuities, you will learn more about their interests in your organization and, more than likely, have a better sense of their overall financial capacities. By paying close attention during the conversations when establishing an annuity, you may learn more about what motivates the donor as well as why they are purchasing the annuity. Record all of this information and use it in follow-up conversations. By so doing, you will be better prepared to speak with your donors and tailor messages about your organization to them. This not only may lead to another gift, but also will enhance your relationship with the donor and create meaningful stewardship over time.

Bequests

Bequests, another planned gift, are addressed in greater depth elsewhere in this volume (see Chapter 6). However, they are an important outcome of mature relationships so should be mentioned here.

A bequest—a gift made through a will—signifies a special relationship with a donor. Bequests are sometimes called legacy gifts, for it is through them that the relationship to the donor lives on in the organization. While the donor's intention always must be respected, the wise organization develops a plan to set aside these gifts to create investments that will yield benefits well into the future. Whether those investments are made in stocks and bonds, real estate, or some other form of long-term investment is not of concern here. Rather, when the bequest is understood as a gift coming from a donor's lifetime of hard work and careful money management, the respectful organization puts it to work for the long-term future, not to take care of immediate needs.

---

*Typically, a bequest comes from someone
who knows you, likes you, knows what you do,
and likes what you do.*

Customarily, only request a bequest after a donor has established a solid, long-term relationship with your organization. The likely donors who will remember your organization in their wills are those who gave regularly over the years (though not necessarily always in very large amounts) and who probably contributed major gifts to capital campaigns or other similar appeals. Typically, a bequest comes from someone who truly knows you, likes you, knows what you do, and likes what you do.

Ask for bequests quietly throughout the year. The wise organization regularly publishes articles about donors who have told the organization that it has been included in their wills. Similarly, including reminders about the organization's willingness to accept bequests (is there an organization that doesn't want one of these gifts?) in newsletters, magazines, bulletins, on the organization website, and even in email signature lines all are subtle reminders to the donors to remember your organization when doing estate planning.

However, do not be lulled into thinking that this passive approach is sufficient. It is not. While many people's bequests come as a surprise to the organization, the wise organization actively solicits bequests as part of its overall development plan. There are several strategies to consider, including the passive one described above.

As your organization identifies its regular and major donors, consider an annual mailing designed to do little more than to make this subset of your donors aware of your willingness to accept their bequest. Days or seasons that are significant to your work are good opportunities for such a mailing. For example, Catholic organizations might schedule a mailing (whether postal or electronic) to coincide with the feast of All Saints Day (November 1) and All Souls Day (November 2). This time of year is a natural one for recalling the impermanence of human life. Preparing for one's death is a part of the human journey. Preparing one's will is as well. Connecting your organization's invitation to leave a legacy gift to a time of year when the calendar and your work coincide may make for greater success.

Be aware, of course, that not everyone is focused on the same thing. Some of your donors are facing other challenges and are attracted by other things. This invitation may not be timed right for them, which is why the message "remember us in your will" must be kept before them through more subtle means (as stated above).

In addition to this annual communication requesting a legacy gift, your organization will benefit from a plan to solicit directly bequests from donors. Ideally, making this request at a time when the donor is writing a will for the first time or revising it would be best; yet, this is not something the typical donor announces. By having established a mature relationship with a donor, however, you can ask when it would be a good time to propose a bequest. Or, you can simply make a request so that the donor can consider it. Tailor that request to the donor's interests and how they connect to your organization. Asking for a legacy gift so that a specific part or program of your organization's activities about which the donor cares can continue well into the future should not come as a surprise to the donor. Rather, through the process of deepening the relationship with the donor, the wise development director has a clear understanding of what will motivate the donor to give a legacy gift based on a well-crafted, well-timed request.

Bequests should, over time,
become a regular source of income.

The above assumes the simple bequest; that is, a donor names your organization in his or her will for either a specific amount or a percentage of the estate. Typically, there is little for the organization to do to receive a gift from a donor's estate. Of course, sometimes wills are contested. When this happens it may make for complications with the donor's family or some other beneficiary. While attorneys often advise their clients to notify family members of the contents of their wills before their deaths, this does not always happen. It is best to be prepared for a contested will.

In the same way that the annual appeal or its equivalent is the foundation of your organization's fundraising, bequests should, over time, become a regular source of income. This will happen if your organization develops a culture of philanthropy designed to include bequests. Gifts from estates do not have to be very large. I have been part of organizations that received $10,000 from estates worth several million dollars. The gift (bequest) is often made in proportion to the size of the receiving organization. Consider what it would mean if your organization annually received several bequests each totaling no more than $10,000. While gifts much larger than this are possible, I consider these $10,000 and smaller bequests to be the bread and butter of a planned-giving strategy. Many of your organization's donors are able to make a bequest of this size while also providing for their families and other organizations. A $10,000 gift might never have been possible during the donor's lifetime, but bequests come from accumulated assets making what seemed impossible very possible.

I suspect if the parish had asked, my parents would have included it in their will.

Let me end this section with a personal story. My parents died in the mid-1980s, about a year apart. They had written their wills several years prior to their deaths—in fact, at the time my brother married. (Pay attention to life events in your donor's lives.) My brother and I were their sole named heirs. At the time of their deaths, we both were well-employed, living comfortable lives. Their estate was quite simple and, after paying final bills, each of us received half of their estate. Without revealing too much information, suffice it to say it was not a life-changing amount of money.

We were, of course, thankful for the gift. At the same time, neither of us would have missed it if we had received $5,000 less. However, their parish, in which they had been very active members, would surely have noticed a check for $10,000. Apparently the parish never asked them for a bequest. My parents evidently never thought of it or any other charity. They were not wealthy, but they had enough to leave something to their children (my brother and me). Why not leave something to their parish? They had given weekly for many years and contributed to building funds and other special fundraising efforts. I suspect if the parish had asked, my parents would have included it in their will.

This is one example of the missed opportunity. A disciplined organization can build a reserve fund and eventually an endowment by passively and actively soliciting bequests. By getting used to doing this with people of moderate means, the organization can prepare to ask with confidence its more affluent donors for more sizeable gifts made through their wills or other devices.

Complex Planned Gifts

Trusts

Wealthier donors to your organization typically have more complicated wills and estates than most people do. Through the creation of trusts, wealthier people avoid the payment of estate and other taxes and place restrictions on their assets both during their lifetimes and after their deaths. The director of development of a small-to-average sized organization is not likely to be able to advise a donor regarding the structuring of trusts and other complex systems used, since this expertise is highly specialized. However, that director should be familiar with various types of trusts and other mechanisms employed to structure giving in a way that protects the donor's assets and interests.

Larger organizations (hospitals, universities, and the like) typically employ people who have the legal and accounting knowledge-base to more fully understand these tools. Whether your organization is large or small, having access to professionals who can advise you and your donor is important. While complex gifts are not likely to become a regular funding source for every organization, the donors who typically use them are very wealthy. By properly positioning your organization and cultivating relationships with wealthy donors, your organization may benefit from a large amount made possible through a complex planned gift.

Access to professionals who can advise you and your donor is important.

Getting over the anxiety of asking for a large gift is a matter of practice. The same thing is true of getting past what might seem a natural fear of the wealthy, who seem to live in a different world than most of us. Do not let television's images of wealth and power cloud your thinking here. Wealthy people are people. The gaps between the experience of those of wealth and those of more moderate or lesser means can be reduced by focusing on the person who has feelings, interests, and concerns just like everyone else. Cultivating a relationship with a person of great wealth is no different than cultivating any other. By paying attention to details and focusing on the interests of the person, the organization will be able to ask for and receive both major and planned gifts.

A Success Story

Having shared here how I wish I had done things differently with my housing organization, let me include a story about a time when things went very well.

While assigned to a downtown parish in Denver, Colorado, I had occasion to develop a relationship with a man who had been a supporter of that parish's ministry to homeless men and women. He was not a parishioner. In fact, he wasn't Catholic. He had moved from Denver to a distant city but still supported the ministry with generous checks.

Good fundraiser that I am, I would call him to thank him when his check arrived.

Through these phone calls we got to know each other a bit. This set the stage for me to ask for an endowment gift. You see, the parish's ministry to the homeless was well known in the city and many people contributed to it. But, I knew that there were peaks and valleys to both income and expenses. A permanent, steady source of funding would help make things work more smoothly. I knew that this man had been a very successful businessman and was quite wealthy. I also knew he was of advanced age so might not live much longer. And, he cared deeply about the homeless.

He was thrilled when I asked if he would consider funding a permanent endowment.

Instead of waiting for another check to arrive to give me the excuse to call him, I simply called him. He told me he took the call because he assumed we were out of funds and needed him to send a check, something he would gladly have done. But, he was thrilled when I asked if he would consider funding a permanent endowment. Without giving him a moment to think beyond that, having prepared well for this call, I was about to ask him for one million dollars. Instead I asked him for two million. And he said yes. Two days later I was on a conference call with him and his estate planners. The money would be held in the foundation to be established upon his death, designated for the perpetual support of the parish's ministry to the homeless. He was delighted to know his giving would outlast his time on this planet. We, of course, were very grateful.

Not every major or planned gift I have helped negotiate has been that easy. But I smile every time I visit Denver and see homeless people going into and out of that church. The donor has since passed away, but the sandwiches, socks, and support the homeless receive are made possible, in part, by his very generous bequest.

Mature Development Strategy

The biographies and writings of St. Vincent de Paul are filled with information about how he went about raising funds for the Congregation of the Mission, its works, and those of other organizations he founded or helped found. Vincent saw so much that needed to be done. Perhaps this is why he founded more than one organization. Did he realize that all the world's ills would need more than even the united and focused efforts of one organization? Or, was it a matter of wanting to be able to engage in mission more people than any one organization could accommodate? Whatever the motivation, it serves as an example of something of which we need to be aware and to which we need to be responsive today.

Our donors are our partners in mission.

While the needs of our organizations surely motivate us to seek gifts of many sizes and types, it is important for us not to lose sight of Vincent's call to engage others in our mission. Financial contributions of any type and size are signs of engagement. Recognizing and acknowledging that our donors are our partners in mission moves the relationship from one of ask-response to an entirely new level.

Questions for Discussion

1. What are our organization's success stories? What are mine?

2. How good are we at "thinking big" as the author suggests?

3. Are we focused on stewardship (our organization) or on the steward (the donor)? Do we need to refocus?

4. Are we developing personal relationships with our donors? Am I? Who can we think of who needs an invitation to make a major gift?

5

Building Bridges, Making Compost

BILL AND MARY FRANCES JASTER

Love is creative even to infinity.
—Vincent de Paul

VINCENT DE PAUL was a bridge-builder. He took ideas from others to inspire his followers. His mission to serve inspires us.

We have witnessed many young people catching that spirit of mission over the years. We begin this chapter about supporting youth as Vincentian Volunteers with the words of twentieth-century internationally renowned priest and author Henri Nouwen about building relationships, believing in a vision, and inviting others to invest their gifts—time, energy, prayers, and cash:

> Fundraising is precisely the opposite of begging. . . . We are not saying, "Please can you help us out because lately it's been hard." Rather, we are declaring that we have a vision that is amazing and exciting. We are inviting you to invest yourself through the resources that God has given you—your energy, your prayers, and your money—in this work to which God has called us.

Colorado Vincentian Volunteers

This is the story about the Colorado Vincentian Volunteers (CVV). But it is more than that. It is about a community of believers. It is about building bridges between young and old. It is about a Vincentian vision of companionship with the poor. It is about "turning compost into fertile soil" and developing the resources necessary for a Vincentian volunteer mission sustained over time. We present the continuing story of developing a support system for young people who give a year of service as they prepare for the next steps of their lives—journeys that then lead them to a life of service with a Vincentian spirit in their own communities.

With the Congregation of the Mission of the Midwest Province, we formed CVV in 1994. We had spent 20+ years as youth ministers, initiating and implementing a youth urban retreat, and working with agencies that serve the poor. During this time, two needs became clear:

- Local, nonprofit agencies serving the poor were having trouble finding and keeping qualified and affordable staff.
- Young adults, especially those in the 22–30 age range, were looking for concrete ways of serving the poor and reflecting on these experiences both in terms of faith and life choices.

CVV, with consultation from local nonprofits and others, responded to these needs by developing a program with these offerings:

- Reduced-cost staffing to help local nonprofit agencies serve the poor.
- Structured, faith-centered opportunities to help young adults to serve the poor.

Since 1994, CVV has annually recruited 12–20 young adults, primarily recent college graduates, from throughout the United States to participate in the program. These volunteers agree to spend a year at Denver nonprofit agencies serving the poor full-time. They live in community, integrating their service experiences through a yearlong spiritual formation program including prayer, retreats, mentoring, and regular theological reflection.

From 1995 to 2012, 217 volunteers completed the program, providing over 60 local nonprofit agencies with more than 375,000 hours of volunteer service. CVV volunteers provided savings to those agencies of $3,900,000 in salary and benefits.

Community of Believers

CVV's beginnings were in 1994, when, because of declining enrollments, St. Thomas Seminary (Denver) was closing. Friends of the seminary paid attention, listened, and offered help in a variety of ways. It is funny to remember the sticky notes our team placed on furniture throughout the seminary after it closed—sticky notes claiming the sofa, bed, dresser, and coffee table as the first donations to the CVV house on Pearl Street. Soon young adults would move in, volunteers giving to the world because of their commitment to justice and service. The sale of the assets from a seminary for Catholic priests would help establish a house of common life and work for young men and women.

The story doesn't end there. A local donor had wanted to make a gift to the seminary, as he believed in the formation of young men preparing for a life of service. But, since the seminary was closing, his gift anonymously shifted to CVV. Our board president (a Vincentian priest and former real estate agent) worked with the donor, with us, and with the housing market of Denver. We used the gift as a down payment to purchase the present CVV home.

People invested through their God-given resources.

Shortly after making the down payment, two more collaborators created CVV's first fundraiser—a breakfast at the Brown Palace Hotel hosted by our board attorney's law firm and a local pastor and friends. Breakfast brought us $28,000 and a new board member: one life touching another, touching another.

Our house needed more beds. Friends, family, and people from a network of local parishes responded; several families volunteered to sponsor a bedroom to complete the furnishings. The vision of a group of young people working and living the Vincentian spirit was amazing and exciting. People invested through their God-given resources—time, energy, prayer, money, and then dressers, lamps, and desks.

Community of Bridging Old and Young

> Your sons and daughters will prophesy, your young men will see visions, your old men will dream dreams. (Acts of the Apostles, 2:17.)

The CVV's experience of support crosses cultural and age boundaries, but we found a surprising pattern over the years of older people intrigued by young adults committing themselves to serving those in need. These young volunteers are signs of hope to their elders—hope for the future, hope as future leaders, hope for an age when bad news is prevalent. The older community members share in the service vicariously.

Our young adults inspire older generations who wish they had had a similar opportunity to volunteer. The young adults inspire with their energy, enthusiasm, idealism, and positive outlook. They inspire not only by their service at their worksites, but also by their commitment to raise funds through fundraising events. They inspire grandchildren of the older generation to volunteer and carry on. Similarly, the elders' wisdom, longevity, commitment, and openness to change inspire the younger volunteers. The bridge between old and young forge experiences of CVV as seen in the following stories.

In the early 1990s, we shared our ideas with the Vincentian priests who listened to the dream and connected it with their own plan, Vision 2000. They realized the need to carry on the lifework of Vincent de Paul even while their ranks were diminishing. What better way to pass on the values, virtues, and commitment to the poor than to embrace young people with a hope to serve and a vision to be open to learning more about Vincent and the Vincentian values?

What better way to pass on the values, virtues, and commitment of your organization than to embrace young volunteers?

The Vincentians embraced the idea and supported us financially, most substantially in the first three crucial years of the program's initial stages, but always with the expressed intent that CVV would gather local support and become self-sufficient. This became a reality in the fifth year, requiring the creation of committees for the board of directors: program, management, and development and public relations. We invited a Sister of Charity who had dedicated her life to education as teacher, principal, and development director to be part of the development committee. Over and over, she encouraged us while also assisting by writing grants and leading our development efforts.

One day a group of retired parishioners were chatting after their adult-education session at the parish. They said, "How about we start an auxiliary to help CVV raise funds? It will be a 'companion' organization; a group building bridges and working with finances, but that never has to have a meeting."

Thus began the Companions of Colorado Vincentian Volunteers, who over the years have planned fundraising events, solicited corporations and small businesses to donate hats, sweaters, gloves, food, school supplies, and so on for the agencies where our volunteers work. Rarely do they have a meeting, as they are too busy doing rather than talking about it.

What do we do about the day-to-day needs of a small nonprofit on a limited budget? We tell our story wherever we can, sharing the passion of vision and mission in parishes, at senior groups, at St. Vincent de Paul Society meetings, at civic groups, and with people who want to be involved. Retired men have consistently appeared at our doors to fix a leaky faucet, mend a chair, repair an old sprinkler system, or varnish a peace pole. Women have come to clean in readiness for a new group, lick envelopes on mailings, deliver bread, file papers, and make copies for retreat programs. Community support of this kind is another bridge—one that is not always measured monetarily.

Support comes by different means from connections within the community and in ways beyond cash donations. Prayer families support volunteers not only by praying for them throughout the year, but also by extending their homes to volunteers adjusting to a new city.

Companionship with the Poor

Companion means "together with bread." How do we break and make bread together at the same time as we engage one another with Vincentian values? As the volunteers companion with the poor, they reflect on those experiences—theologically—and then share stories through our newsletter published three times per year. The newsletter has become an important source of income as well as a link between the volunteers' experiences and those who believe in and support CVV.

Those who receive the newsletter love hearing the reflections and stories of the volunteers.

We have a staff member who edits stories written by the volunteers. A local graphic designer does the layout, and we have the newsletter printed at a discount at a local printing company. It's available on our website, and we also mail to a list of supporters—friends and family members of staff and volunteers. Since we focus on volunteers' experiences, the newsletter becomes a source of income and public relations. Over and over we hear that those who receive it love hearing the reflections and stories of the volunteers. At the end of the year, volunteers also write a story as part of the closing retreat. Not unlike the way Vincent used to share stories so as to share his mission and attract people and resources, these stories share the CVV mission, attracting people and resources. This is one of those stories.

When I first met Paula, a beneficiary of the program, she already carried her oxygen tank in her cart. She had not yet taken to wearing medical masks to workshop, but you could tell she was physically weak, devastated by the cancer ravaging her body. She often showed up a few minutes late for reflection on workshop days, but I never reprimanded her, knowing her physical limitations—she could hardly walk to the garden, impeded by her oxygen tank and a limp in her gait.

When she showed up, Paula made her presence known. She liked to talk, to put it nicely. She was often rude to other participants or staff, seemed overly willing to share opinions or experiences, and often complained loudly about the pain she was going through and how difficult her life was.

It was easy to turn a blind eye to Paula, to dismiss her because of her unpleasant demeanor, or to ignore the pain she was feeling physically and emotionally. She represents the "less attractive" side of poverty—showing the ugly realities of homelessness, illness, and mental-health issues. Because of all this, at first I kept a certain distance from her. I was at times short with her, half ignoring what she said to me, hoping her conversations in the workshop would end before they got long. She was not a priority for me. I didn't give her the fullness of my respect.

One day during group reflection, though, after a particularly tough stretch of doctors' visits, exams, and rounds of chemo, Paula broke down under the weight of her situation. She cried as she described what she was going through. One of the volunteers asked if there were anything the reflection group could do to support her. Paula simply replied, "I could use some hugs."

At first no one stepped forward to meet her opened arms. Then one moved in, and then another. I sat for a moment hesitating. It made me feel upset, embarrassed, and ashamed that I was so distant from her that I questioned even hugging her in this moment of need. I put those thoughts aside, stood up, and walked over to hug her as she cried. As I held her I told her, "We care so much about you, Paula." Sitting back down, I realized that this was what she needed all along—the warm embrace of community. She may have appeared to me to be desperate for attention, but she was really desperate for connection, for love, for hope.

She may have appeared desperate for attention, but she was really desperate for connection, for love, for hope.

I still sometimes have to push past feelings of being annoyed or bothered by her behavior in workshop, but the most overwhelming feeling I have for Paula now is love. Unconditional, even in the midst of ugliness. Unconditional, because that's what Paula deserves.

Conclusion: Turning Compost into Fertile Soil

We need to be good compost piles. We gather leftovers which become fertile soil. Then we spread it where it's needed. (Former volunteer.)

At times we have hit the wall with fundraising, especially in regards to grants from foundations or events that take more work than results show. This raw compost becomes fertile ground when we are able to raise friends as much as funds or introduce the mission to an individual who, though part of another foundation, is willing to support in other ways.

Compost piles start as stinky, ugly, messy globs of moldy and rotting raw vegetables. Later, when mixed with dry organic matter and water, with enough time, heat and air—all acting together—the rot is transformed into a mature compost of rich, dark, organic matter, now fertile soil for growth. It is not only about sustaining life, but also about planting seeds in that rich soil—seeds that will blossom at a later time.

Here is our recipe for "compost" to develop and sustain youth as activists and volunteers. Start with simple ingredients and raw materials: young adults willing to offer time, energy, education, enthusiasm, idealism, hope, and curiosity. Include their search for spirituality and meaning and their willingness to walk with the poor, live in community, and grow spiritually for a year of their lives. Add staff and community volunteers committed to engage them throughout the year and a spiritual formation program to guide both.

Next add the "organic matter": a vision and mission, a committed and inspired board of directors, the experienced hands of those with lifelong similar values, development directors from local agencies, and local adults involved with the organization on a grassroots level. These ingredients provide the knowledge, experience, wisdom, and guidance to ignite the support needed over time.

Water is imperative; whether in a humid or dry climate, our compost needs moisture. This ingredient helps expand the support of our compost (program). It includes: sharing the organization's story through fundraisers, friend-raisers, grant writing, the Internet, local newspapers, newsletters, and other publications; speaking to groups about the vision and mission; involving alumni on the board and committees; evaluating the program; calling upon local businesses to support the work; gleaning what is needed to sustain the program (food, office supplies, printing, household items, building materials, etc.), which also engages the broader community in the mission.

Mix, allow the materials to intermingle, breathe, and cook. Vincent spoke of this when he said, "If we are really called to carry the love of God far and wide, if we are to enflame the nations with this fire, if we have the vocation of setting the whole world on fire, if it is so, I say, if it is so, my brothers, then how much I must myself burn with the divine fire." It takes our fire and passion for the mission to ignite the energy that will transform these simple ingredients into fertile soil that is sustainable over time.

Finally, allow time to create the rich matter. This result requires patience, commitment, discipline, and a willingness to allow the other ingredients to transform into something new, sustainable, and always growing and changing. Then, we begin again, time after time, year after year, with a new group, new budget, new partners to find, and new fundraiser to plan. The stability of that compost pile will give energy to the process. We continue to believe what Nouwen said and what Vincent demonstrated: "We are declaring that we have a vision that is amazing and exciting. We are inviting you to invest yourself through the resources that God has given you—your energy, your prayers, and your money—in this work to which God has called us."

Questions for Discussion

1. What are the ingredients needed to sustain our organization's mission and vision over time? How do we keep the compost fertile?

2. How does our mission and vision promote a vocation to a life of service?

3. What are the needs of our community? The young people? What is the connection between the two?

4. Who are our organization's companions?

6
The Vincentian Mission and the Bequest
CHARLES F. SHELBY, C.M.

All we have to do is walk straight ahead and do well to make everyone our friend.
—Vincent de Paul

Why Have a Will?

WHEN I first started at DePaul University as vice chancellor, I interviewed a few alumni who had small giving histories but had the capacity for larger gifts. The first person I spoke with was a semi-retired judge. I interviewed him in his office in the Federal Courthouse. Among my questions was, "Do you have a will?"

"No," he said.

"May I ask why?"

"I'm not going to die."

I gave him a moment to think of what he had just said. He was a judge, an alumnus of DePaul's College of Law. He realized quickly, "Well, I guess I am not immortal." I suggested that he give the matter more thought and then act on it—and to please keep DePaul in mind.

Surprisingly, the judge was in the majority. According to the survey, "A Study about Estate Planning," by Harris Interactive for LexisNexis

Martindale-Hubbell (April 2004), 55 percent of Americans do not have a will. If you do not have a will, the state steps in and provides the service when you pass. The exact amounts vary from state to state, but in general the state will divide your assets among immediate family members according to fixed formulas. If you want anything else at all, you must have a will (or technically, an estate plan, which would include a will, a trust, or another vehicle to express and determine what you wish to do with your assets at death).

Why Do People Give Charitable Bequests?

A charitable bequest is a gift of personal property by will to a legal charity. People make bequests such as these in order to control how much and which of their assets go to various people and organizations.

Often a person has developed charitable habits by becoming involved in the causes, works, and organizations in which he or she believes. A charitable bequest, put simply, allows the donor's involvement in that cause to continue even after death.

Types of Bequests

There are several types of bequests. The definitions are provided here for the reader's convenience.

- **Bequest, simple bequest, or legacy.** A gift by will, especially of money or personal property.
- **Residuary bequest.** A gift by will from the property that remains after all other gifts in the will have been satisfied.
- **Trust.** A fiduciary relationship in which one person (the trustee) holds the legal title to property (the trust property) subject to an obligation to keep or use the property for the benefit of another person (the beneficiary). The trust agreement describes the obligations of the trustees and their successors. In terms of estate planning, the trustee, while alive and capable,

manages and disposes of the property. After the trustee's death, the trust agreement determines how the property is distributed under management of the successor trustee. In practical effect, the trust works like a will but is free from the restrictions of estate laws.

- **Annuity.** The amount payable according to contract or trust annually or at other regular intervals for either a certain or an indefinite period. An "annuitant" is another name for the beneficiary of an annuity. A charitable gift annuity is an annuity issued by a charity. At the annuitant's death, the charity retains the balance of the funds in the annuity for its charitable purposes.
- **Charitable remainder trust.** A tax-exempt irrevocable trust designed to reduce individual taxable income by first dispersing income to the trust beneficiaries for a specified period of time and then donating the remainder of the trust to the designated charity.

The Significance of a Bequest

Another meaning of the term "legacy" is "something transmitted by or received from an ancestor or predecessor or from the past." In this sense, a legacy is something for which someone might want to be remembered, a living monument to the good a person has done in life. It also serves as a way to continue the person's good works after death.

There is a saying, "You can't take it with you." This was once depicted by the image of a hearse pulling a trailer.

As someone engaged in development, however, I prefer the saying, "You can't take it with you, but you can send it on ahead." In other words, whatever advantage you gain by doing good while on earth can endure after your death by leaving a bequest to continue doing good in your name.

Joking aside, it is a common wish to live on beyond death through our actions. Establishing a memorial through a charitable organization accomplishes that. We see numerous examples, such as establishing an endowment, or donating a building or part of a building.

The Association of the Miraculous Medal

The Association of the Miraculous Medal in Perryville, Missouri, promotes devotion to Mary the Mother of God, offers pastoral care to its members, and supports the works of the Vincentian priests and brothers in the western United States and Kenya. Members of the Association are ordinary Catholics, and they rely on the Association to reach out to them especially when the needs are great in times of suffering. The Vincentians the Association supports work with the neglected and underprivileged.

A devoted member left the Association a four-figure bequest. His wife still corresponds with the Association. Here is their story, as published in the Association's bulletin in December 2011. At the end is an example of a gentle offer of information about creating one's own bequest.

Michael "Mike" Korchak was born on October 24, 1923, in Star Junction, Pennsylvania. Raised and educated in Brooklyn, New York, Mike served his country in the United States Navy during World War II. After the war, he worked as a merchant seaman for 10 years before going to work for the Brooklyn Union Gas Company as a gas line repairman. He retired after 25 years of service to the company.

He married Mary Agnes Reynolds on October 4, 1958. They lived in North Bend, Oregon. Michael's life was one of simplicity. He took great pleasure from helping others. He spent many happy hours working at the local food bank. He loved to fish, and enjoyed meeting his friends for coffee on Saturday mornings.

The Virgin Mary played a very important role in Michael's life. He and Mary Agnes recited the rosary together every morning until he was no longer able to do so. He carried his rosary with him everywhere he went.

On October 18, 2010, Michael passed away. The Association of the Miraculous Medal was blessed with the friendship of Michael and Mary Agnes for more than thirty years. At the time of Michael's death, [AMM] received a generous bequest from his estate.

Send for our free brochure, "Your Estate Plan—4 Easy Steps." It is designed to help you begin the process of making an orderly distribution of your property in a manner that will accomplish your estate planning objectives and continue your legacy of charitable giving to our Lady's Association through your will.

Learn how you can become a member of Mary's Legacy Society by remembering our Lady's Association in your will. Or contact our Planned Giving Coordinator for more information about planning your estate. Please consider making a gift to the Association of the Miraculous Medal in your will.

DePaul University

The following example illustrates how the Vincentian mission influenced the donor of the bequest and then later the successor trustees to direct the entire bequest to DePaul University (provided by Joel Schaffer, assistant vice president, planned giving, DePaul University). It also is a reminder that recognition of the donor by naming a building or a program is an appropriate way to express appreciation for a gift, which in this case was seven figures. It shows that a financial and planned giving advisor can have a positive influence on a gift.

Charles Kellstadt was a well-respected businessman in Chicago who retired as chairman of Sears at the end of his career. He and his wife created a charitable trust (foundation) in 1975 that was to run for twenty-five years. Charles was particularly interested in urban higher education and Catholic institutions. During the term of the trust, the foundation made annual grants to organizations of higher education in the Chicago area. There were three trustees of the foundation, two of whom were not Catholic. As the foundation neared the period for final distribution of the principal of the trust, various organizations in competition for disposition of the trust approached the trustees.

Ed Brennan, a former chairman of Sears and chairman of the DePaul University Board of Trustees came to the three trustees with a proposal for the funds. The trustees ultimately decided to make the gift to DePaul University as its mission was closest to the vision of Charles Kellstadt. At the time, it was the largest single gift that DePaul University had ever received in its history. Today the Kellstadt Graduate School of Business at DePaul University has a number of high-ranking programs that are recognized worldwide.

One of the former trustees explained to DePaul's planned giving officer this story of how she was able to come to a decision on final distribution of the trust's funds. She is proud of her efforts on behalf of DePaul University and the students whose lives it transforms year in and year out.

Attracting Gifts through Mission

Every organization should have its own mission statement, so that benefactors can know to what kind of organization they are donating. The statement should be a brief and direct description of the organization's unique mission—its purpose, its stakeholders, and how it accomplishes its purpose. It should inspire everyone who hears or sees it, including (especially for our purpose) prospective donors. One measure of the effectiveness of a mission statement is whether it attracts donors to a charitable organization.

The Vincentian mission—to reach out with compassion serving people's basic needs and to address systemically the challenges and causes of poverty—is not specific to any particular organization but is shared by many organizations that make it specific according to their own identity.

Questions for Discussion

1. Let's start in the beginning: Does everyone in our organization have a will? Are they up to date?

2. Why would people put off drafting a will? What fears and decisions can our organization help them face?

3. Vincent lived almost 80 years. He gave all his savings to the poor when he founded his organizations—long before he died. The good he did lives on throughout the world 400 years later. What good will live on after our donors pass?

7

A Personal Story of Vincentian Philanthropy

J. PATRICK MURPHY, C.M.

*You will see a great amount of misery that you cannot
relive. . . . Share their trials with them; do all you can to provide
them with a little assistance and remain at peace.*
—Vincent de Paul

J. PATRICK MURPHY interviewed Bill and Mary Pat Hay on February 22, 2011, about their personal approach to philanthropy. Their responses illustrate their own values and how they match up with traditional Vincentian and DePaul University values.

Murphy: When did you make your first gift to DePaul?

Bill: Our first gift to DePaul was many years ago—thirty years ago—when I belonged to the DePaul President's Club. We donated $1,000 during the year and in turn we got invited to the spring student symphony.

Mary Pat: It was like being struck by a lightning bolt seeing the kids on stage. It was like looking at a mini-United Nations with students of every race, creed, and color playing their hearts out. They were fabulous. I just fell in love with DePaul at that moment.

Bill: I used to always say to Vaughn Dann [DePaul associate vice president for development], we really need to do something with these events. They need an afterglow with music and dancing where people can stick around for a cocktail and connect with the University.

Mary Pat: The symphony is a great time for this because it allows us to see our product, which are these talented, beautiful young people playing magnificently. It is awesome.

Bill: As Dennis [Reverend Dennis Holtschneider, C.M., president of the University] used to say: "You won't just hear notes today, you will hear their hopes, dreams, and aspirations."

Murphy: What motivated you to make that first gift or a gift?

Bill: As an alumnus of DePaul, I've always believed it was my duty to give back to the University. I warmed up to DePaul and what they had done for me. As a full-time faculty member for five years and part-time for thirty years, I felt increased kinship with the institution that was a springboard to our success in business and life. In contrast, my other alma mater never asked me for money. I fell through the cracks—as if they didn't know I existed. I gave $100 once and now I just ignore them. DePaul had it right. I became friends with Vaughn Dann through DePaul and after joining the President's Club, Vaughn sought us out for lunch with her and Father Cortelyou [Reverend John R. Cortelyou, C.M., the eighth president of DePaul, 1964 to 1981].

Mary Pat: Father Cortelyou was charming and interesting; together they were a great tag team.

Bill: My appreciation for the school has not been linear—I have had ups and downs with DePaul. I have been fiercely angry at DePaul over some things—a termination, the treatment of a revered faculty member. I didn't understand why, so my contributions waned during those times.

"The Church over the centuries has been a force for good—missionary work, hospitals, teaching, healing the sick, offering comfort, helping the poor."

Mary Pat: We eventually stepped up to the plate again. During a meeting with Jack Minogue [former president of DePaul], he mentioned that Vincentians were going the way of the buffalos. So we wondered who would be there to carry Vincentian values forward. This came at a time of my renewed involvement with the Catholic Church. I now have a profound belief that the Church over the centuries has been a force for good—missionary work, hospitals, teaching, healing the sick, offering comfort, helping the poor. Vincent was the poster child for that. We started asking who would carry these ideals forward. This is when we started talking about funding a program of people with Vincentian ideals, going into communities and providing the same type of services Vincent did—healing the sick, feeding the poor, doing all the things he did so masterfully.

Murphy: Why have you fallen in love with DePaul?

Bill: All my life I have felt like DePaul was a family. It was hard to get away from. People who have worked here their entire lives would testify to this. They may have considered leaving at certain times, but they never could. When push came to shove, they realized they loved the people too much. These are secretaries, administrative staff, faculty, deans—all levels. There is a wonderful feeling of bonding and camaraderie. This may be because of DePaul's religious affiliation, but its smallness contributes, too. With that comes periods of disagreements, but there is a great environment to voice opinion and live to talk about it.

This atmosphere has continued on the board. For instance, there is a current dispute over the conflict of interest policy. I called Dennis and voiced my opinion. This is a great family we have going on here, which allows us to talk about things and come up with solutions. As furious as I sometimes get with DePaul responses, I still want to be a part of it and continue to contribute. Mary Pat's involvement with the School of Music has further solidified that bonding with the University; her perceptions have in turn fueled my continued interest in it.

Mary Pat: During the recent public kick-off of our capital campaign, students joined in explaining how Vincentian values aligned with their own. A student with her headscarf said she is a "Muslim Vincentian." We hope that is what the Vincent Leadership Project is all about.

Bill: Pat [Patricia O'Donoghue, vice president for alumni affairs] once told me that the contribution rate among alumni at DePaul is about 6 percent; Loyola is about 9 percent, Northwestern and the University of Illinois are higher, and Notre Dame is in the 40–50 percent range—and we wondered why. For starters, we haven't moved DePaul to the middle of some cornfield [as have other schools in the state]. When you cluster people for four years, they become brainwashed. The school becomes their religion, their dogma. At DePaul, it is a different collegiate experience. Students tend to close the door and don't look back. We need to work on that.

Murphy: What types of values, religious or otherwise, are behind your giving?

Mary Pat: I live according to the Golden Rule: do unto others as you would have them do unto you. I also believe in the Beatitudes, and this motivates my charitable giving. I think we must help people who need help. Part of that is training people in universities to go out and help people.

Bill: I think education is the passport out for kids growing up today. They can't use just any springboard to improve their lives. Without education, they are relegated to a totally different life. If their gifts result in allowing people to further their education, so be it. When I walk down Monroe Street [in Chicago] and I see my favorite panhandler with his cup, I am very conflicted. I know that Darrel goes right out and buys a bottle or takes a pill. But I feel compelled to give, to help.

A friend of ours had it right: just give it to them and shut up about it. You've got what they need, and you don't need it, so give it to them and shut up. I often think of a friend who, when coming off the expressway at the stoplight on North Avenue, sees the guy with a cardboard sign working the cars. He digs down into his pocket and gives him a $20. When I asked him why he gives so much money, he told me, "Because he might be Jesus." I will never forget that. I thought, *So it is with philanthropy and St. Vincent.* We should spend the rest of our lives giving to the poor what they need—not to our peers, to the poor. I go through this over and over in my mind wondering whether I am just enabling.

Mary Pat: One day I went to the bank and I got $500 in ones. Every time I saw a panhandler I gave him a buck. I don't often give to them, but I thought they're so needy and it's cold, gray, wet, and miserable out there? It might mean everything to them. I know this isn't the way to deal with poverty—the way to deal with it is the Vincentian method as a whole community environment, perhaps through government, where we handle education, housing, health, everything. That's how we should deal with poverty, and that is what I want to see our country address. But we are not yet doing that in a very complete way. So we do it one buck at a time.

Murphy: Why is DePaul worthy of gifts?

Bill: It is all built on personal relationships and a belief in DePaul as stewards of making this happen, of converting dollars that are donated into opportunities for students. Dennis was right: we see aspiration here everywhere, and people want to contribute to that.

"I want our students to embrace [Vincent's] values, and then go forth and do it with their college education."

Mary Pat: I would go beyond saying opportunities for kids. Another motivation is to create opportunities for students to live the life that Vincent taught us in caring for others.

Bill: It is about having a personal relationship with Vincent himself.

90

Mary Pat: He led the way in so many ways teaching how to take care of the poor, educate them, care for women and children, and provide relief for all kinds of horrible situations back then. I want our students to embrace his values, and then go forth and do it with their college education. They can still do it as an investment banker or a lawyer, they can still take those values into our community—that is important. This is the legacy of Vincent—DePaul doesn't just offer careers, but it educates students with the belief that they must live a life caring for others.

Bill: I believe in the work Laura Hartman [professor of business ethics and management at DePaul] has done on ethics and management. I want to believe DePaul students really know the difference between right and wrong and that this carries forward with them in their careers and lives in this troubled world. I believe Catholics and Protestants grow up with a strong sense of values—knowing what is right and wrong.

"No one sits around in large corporations and thinks about the poor. It is up to individuals to fund this sector."

Murphy: What is the role of the nonprofit sector? Does it influence your opinion of philanthropy?

Bill: Real good in the world is done in the nonprofit sector—not at GM, Cisco, or big companies. The real contributions, other than technological advancement, have been from this sector. No one sits around in large corporations and thinks about the poor. It is up to individuals to fund this sector as the only place where people are really concerned about the poor.

Mary Pat: This is how the Safer Foundation came about. Its founders asked, "If we don't do it, who will? Who is going to pick up that cost?" Only a not-for-profit would do that.

Murphy: Bill, what motivated you to accept the position on DePaul's board?

Bill: I am a governance junkie, and it was always an adventure for me. I was always intrigued about how DePaul operates and functions, and I have always suspected that presidents through the years viewed the board as reporting to them rather than vice versa. Boards were something to be reckoned with—just fundraisers. I thought I had something to contribute. Jack Minogue always fascinated me as something of a rogue president who needed to be corralled; I think he saw that in me.

Mary Pat: I joined the School of Music's board through a friend at the Mercy Home who graduated from the School of Music to become chairman of the board. He knew me to be an event planner and fundraiser and invited me on.

Murphy: What is your role as board member in fundraising?

Bill: The gifts we have given have enabled me to say to my colleagues, "Show me the money." It has worked perfectly—so well that trustees don't want to sit down and talk with me. They just want to send a check; they ask how much I want. I feel trustees ought to belly up to the bar. Some have had a free ride before without contributing anything, but we laid down the law. Lots of trustees left because they would not contribute. They thought they were doing DePaul a favor by being here and lending their name. Now we have people who are interested in good governance and who understand clearly the financial commitment. I can come to them during special campaigns and ask for their help, but everyone has to make a substantial gift on their own.

Mary Pat: I have a slightly different take because every time I worked in fundraising, I believed I was not really asking people for money. I was offering them the opportunity to feel really good about themselves and what they're doing. When I worked development at the Mercy Home, people felt wonderful about giving money to help kids. I feel the same way working for DePaul's performing arts campaign. We are giving people the opportunity to express their appreciation for the arts and help train people who will give continuity to the arts.

Murphy: What tactics do you use to get people to give?

Bill: I ask people to think about making DePaul one of their top three charities. Our board members are very involved in other organizations and their boards, and we are careful about not asking for too much. There is an 80/20 distribution here, with 20 percent of the board doing the heavy lifting in terms of governance—they wind up on the executive committee. But Mary Pat is right, we want to make them feel good about contributing to the University and what they have done. We have not had enough of an educational component to our board meetings—we need to bring in students to connect donors to those who benefit.

Mary Pat: I like to bring people to the spring concert—they see the DePaul orchestra, they write a check. At Mercy Home, I take them to the campus—they tour around, they fall in love. It is like buying a car; the buyer needs to see it. Get the donors on campus at a lecture, a basketball game, anything that will resonate with them. Let them see students in action, feel the excitement, and feel part of it.

Bill: Pat O'Donoghue told me people who attend the first alumni event contribute at the rate of 30–40 percent as opposed to those who never attend an event.

Mary Pat: We need to work our events more and a have a nice social hour that allows people to reconnect with the institution, making it nice for them to be there and worthwhile.

Murphy: Do you make donations as a couple?

Mary Pat: For big donations, we donate as a couple and talk about it, but we both have our own side charities and we do our own things.

Murphy: What legacy would you like to leave?

Bill: Stephen Covey always talked in *The 7 Habits of Highly Effective People* about getting to the end and knowing how you want to be remembered. I think this is so true. I see guys I have worked with who really slip up, and no one will ever remember the good things they did throughout their lifetime. This is what will be written about them. So I want to be known as a decent guy who always tried to do the right thing, and I lived my life according to certain principles. I made a lot of mistakes, but I dusted myself off, tried to keep going, and shared the wealth. I felt passionate about DePaul and other organizations like Mercy.

"So I want to be known as a decent guy who always tried to do the right thing, and I lived my life according to certain principles."

Mary Pat: I want to be remembered as the life of the party and feel very good about how we have contributed. I feel I have covered the bases in terms of what I care about. First, there is Mercy Home and caring for kids who otherwise would not have had a chance. Second is the Vincent on Leadership Project and giving students an opportunity to learn how to take care of others. Third is the DePaul School of Music and the Lyric Opera of Chicago both providing music, which I think is the gateway to the soul. I like the balance of the three things, I am happy about them, and I am thrilled about being able to contribute to all of them. I really want the Hay Leadership project to turn into a total lab experiment for turning out new Vincents. I hope that the kids who benefit from this gift will go forward and do what Vincent did.

Bill: The project is a perfect example of trying to extract what it was about this guy Vincent that made him so effective and how can we shadow him in our lives to replicate that. I like it that he didn't grow up

94

that way. He was kind of an ordinary kid who wouldn't come visit his dad at the seminary. But he then had an epiphany in discovering that his life was all wrong, so he decided to dedicate his life to the poor.

Questions for Discussion

1. Do we know what our major donors think about giving to our mission? Have we ever asked them? Should we?

2. What motivates our donors to give? What motivates me to work for the organization?

3. What are the stories of giving in our organization? Who are heroes? How do we treat them, celebrate them?

8
Moving beyond Rejection

Teresa Manna

It is true that what seems to be a loss, according to the flesh,
is a great advantage according to the spirit and
a great reason to give thanks to God.
—Vincent de Paul

Tom Melohn, best known for acquiring and then revitalizing the company North American Tool and Die in the 1990s, used the mantra "No rejects, no rejects, no rejects!" with his workers. And indeed, over time, they were able to reduce rejected parts from 10 percent to 0.01 percent. That thinking—the pursuit of no rejections—drives American manufacturing. But perhaps it spills over into the business of asking for donations too much.

When we passionately support an ideal or mission, we naturally want others to immediately see its value and join us. Whose mailboxes and inboxes are not flooded with invitations to contribute to XYZ charity, to walk for a cure, to petition a legislator, to attend a golf tournament, to march for life, to donate diapers or dollies, or to pray for one more special intention?

Many accede to one or more of these appeals. More often though, even when we agree with the cause and feel compassion for its beneficiaries, we fail to respond. Depending upon who is asking, we may decline politely with a note or email or simply ignore the invitation altogether.

It is important to keep a balanced perspective on rejection.

Whenever I get turned down it hurts. *Cousin Bobby did not make time to attend the trivia night fundraiser.* But it is important to keep a balanced perspective on rejection. Maybe Bobby had attended numerous charitable events this month, or worked overtime all week, or had not seen his family enough lately.

Only a small percentage of people invited to support an organization or mission will ever do so. According to Mal Warwick, a leading author and consultant in the nonprofit sector, acquisition appeals are losing ventures, typically returning no more than 50–75 percent of the mailing cost and a 1 percent response rate from prospects (Warwick, online article, "How Direct Mail Can Benefit Your Organization").

Once a contributor has come on board, we cannot rest on our laurels. A "one-hit wonder"—a new donor who never gives again—is all too common and inflicts a more personal rejection of our organization or mission. It makes us wonder, "What happened?"

Even more perplexing and unexpected is the long-time advocate who suddenly stops responding. Similarly, what planned giving officer has not experienced the sting of a decisive "no" from a steady contributor who rejects an invitation to make a major or planned gift? Finally, as if ignoring or rejecting our appeals does not set us back enough, we also cope with what many would consider the ultimate expression of donor rejection: "Take my name off your list."

For many who share personally in the mission of the charitable organization for which we work, rejection can sting. Nevertheless, as Vincent de Paul taught us by his own response to failure, we must not retreat in defeat. Rather, we should respond with intention and deliberate action.

"No" can be the best answer.

Is there a redeeming value to rejection? Stories from the field show that "no" can be the best answer and a most-important stepping stone to a better understanding of our donors, our prospects, and even our mission itself. With newfound insights, we can point the way to cultivating more authentic, longer-lasting donor relationships—the foundation of fundraising success.

New Donor as a "One-Hit Wonder"

Nonprofit organizations often find a first-time donor through an acquisition appeal sent to "cold" prospects who contribute to similar organizations and causes. Individual names and addresses can be rented through a list broker for one-time use. The organizations typically anchor the appeal in educating the prospect to one or more tenets of the organization's mission and the difference the work is making in people's lives.

The Congregation of the Mission Western Province (United States), for example, promotes education and formation of clergy and laity, evangelization, pastoral care, and outreach to the poor in Kenya. Recently, a donor gave $100 in response to an acquisition appeal focusing on the mission work. The average gift for first-time contributors to the Province is $13.50, so his gift was significant. Our office responded with the usual follow-up protocol over several months following the initial gift, including a personal thank-you letter, two newsletters, one e-newsletter, one handwritten note, and a set of prayer cards with a letter inviting the donor's prayer intentions.

Six months later, we sent our next appeal, a more general request touching upon the Congregation's broader needs. The new and generous donor did not respond. Because he was unknown to staff and due to the relative generosity of his first gift, we wanted to know why he failed to respond. However, we thought a phone call would be inappropriate. After discussion and reflection, we reasoned he was likely attracted to the work in Kenya as detailed in the initial letter. Was this the mission and message that inspired him?

In a follow-up to that appeal, we segmented this one-time donor alongside other known Kenya donors and personalized the solicitation more narrowly toward the pressing needs among the priests and brothers serving the poor in Kenya. He responded with a second $100 contribution.

Never lose sight of why someone gave in the first place.

The lesson was clear: Never lose sight of why someone gave in the first place. We created a code in the donor gift database that denotes the theme or content of the appeal, and we now track gift dates. In subsequent efforts, we analyze donor response by content or theme rather than as isolated mailings. This quickly revealed the interests of donors contributing to the specific focus.

It would be hard to overstate the value of a first-time donor, especially since two-thirds of them will never give again. Any donor contributing an initial gift of $100 has demonstrated more than a passing interest in the mission. Knowing what moves individual donors to give and strengthening the organization's tie to that passion within them is key to subsequent giving.

As director of the archdiocesan development appeal in St. Louis, I learned a similar lesson when we faced the challenge of finding nearly $400,000 in new monies for the annual campaign.

Having to raise significantly greater pledges in a short time created a panic in operations. We began by meeting personally with our regular, major donors—those having the most generous and steady giving history. I prepared my script to emphasize the need for increased funding for Catholic education. But at one of my earliest meetings, a generous couple who had raised five children flatly rejected "the ask" for an increased donation.

As a mother of two grade-school age children who had benefited tremendously from the priceless gift of our parish school, I was shocked that these parents declined the opportunity to help us meet the needs of the growing cost of Catholic education. However, the failure was mine. None of their youngsters had ever even attended a Catholic school. They live in a good school district and had participated in the parish school of religion. Their generous annual support was inspired by the archdiocese's ongoing work with other causes they cared about.

Had I not been rushed and "pre-programmed" with my campaign-centered case statement, I would have simply asked them why they give to the appeal every year. I would have known what was close to their heart and tailored my remarks more specifically to their priorities.

I moved beyond this rejection by following up with this couple, regularly updating them on programs of interest to them. The following year, having cultivated a more personal relationship, we targeted our solicitation according to their interests. I asked for a $250 increase; they doubled that, adding $500 to their previous giving level.

How to Identify and Build a Major Donor Profile

Your mission will be well served if you identify donors who have given consistently for three or more years. Start building a donor profile that includes:
- Nickname, spouse's name, children's names
- Home address
- Business address, title, work history, financial position

- Affiliations, professional and other clubs, organizations
- Solicitation and giving history for your organization and giving history for other organizations (search online for donors' names, which will often yield annual reports or other donor listings on which they appear)
- Relationships they have within your organization, the history of it and how long it has been, and any other pertinent details
- Interests and views
- Membership on charitable boards, awards received, articles or interviews in periodicals, etc. (search online to discover personal and professional information)

Another great tool for information is the computer database WealthEngine, a research tool to identify major donors and prospects with the ability and propensity to give to your organization. (A free demonstration is available at WealthEngine.com.)

Long-Time Donor Lapses Suddenly

Each spring a large children's service agency in St. Louis hosts a dinner auction. With 400+ donors attending, it is their largest single fundraiser. In a recent year, the charity's development director received no reservation from a major donor who had always attended in the past. When the director phoned the donor to invite her personally, she said that although she loves the agency's mission, she would feel uncomfortable sitting in her customary place at the table of the executive director, a position which had recently changed hands. Evidently, the donor had been closely acquainted with the previous executive director; she did not know the new director nor any other attendees. Politely, she promised to mail a contribution instead.

While not a rejection in a financial sense, here was a potentially huge loss for the agency in terms of an important donor relationship. Of course, this was no one's fault—employees come and go all the time.

However, it points to the reality that fundraising is deeply rooted in personal relationships, something Vincent de Paul knew and used to benefit the Congregation's mission.

Rather than risk further separation, the staff sprang into action. They arranged for the donor to meet with the outgoing and incoming directors at lunch. The woman was touched by the gesture. Feeling more comfortable about the seating arrangement, she attended the event. While seated at the event with the donor, the new executive director worked to get better acquainted. After visiting, the new director invited her to the executive director's table at an upcoming event. She doubled her donation at the auction that year.

Our two lessons here were simple enough.

- **Listen to what is important to the donor.** On the phone, in person, in writing—listen and respond personally. With a little thought and a few phone calls, this perceptive development director averted what might have been a devastating loss of friendship. Instead, out of gratitude and in support of a mission close to her heart, the already-generous donor moved even higher up the giving ladder.

- **People give to people, not causes.** Value the personal relationships that may be motivating a donor's decision to give. As fundraisers, we tend to believe our organization's priorities are donors' priorities. We emphasize mission and vision. We would do better to recognize that many donors may be responding to a single person within the organization who has gained their trust or admiration. The most valuable resources we have in donor cultivation, therefore, might well be our own ministers, staff, and volunteers. It is so often their example and tireless commitment that inspire donors to give. Introduce passionate witnesses to your donors as often as possible.

This intimate connection was at the heart of our founder's most successful fundraising efforts. In Bernard Pujo's spirited biography, we read about Vincent's flair for developing relationships and sharing his vision for God's people in need.

> Vincent had a remarkable tool for raising funds—his outstanding ability to create friendships with all the great families who exercised various kinds of power in the kingdom. From the time of his youth, Vincent had developed this innate gift of being able to arouse the sympathy of those he encountered on his way. (Pujo, p. 106.)

Major Donor Rejects Capital Campaign Request

In 2005, the Vincentian Province in Perryville, Missouri launched a capital campaign to build the Apostle of Charity Residence for senior priests and brothers. With provincial development efforts in their earliest stages, the potential major donors (excluding Congregation members) numbered around twenty-five.

They knew us; they liked us; they knew what we do;
they liked what we do.

Comprising this intimate group were men and women who had grown close to the Vincentians by various associations. Some had been seminarians taking classes and spiritual direction from members. Others had worked in a Vincentian apostolate. Several were close family members. Simply put: they knew us; they liked us; they knew what we do; they liked what we do. Because their interests and relationship with the Vincentians are so well known to us, they became excellent prospects for a capital campaign pledge.

Two rejections surfaced from the group when invited to contribute to the campaign. The first might seem to be an unavoidable coincidence of bad timing: the couple's parish had just kicked off a capital campaign.

Our prospect and his wife had recently made a substantial pledge and were serving as campaign co-chairs. As a result, their gift to the Province campaign was only a small fraction of our expectation.

One might assume this could not be helped. However, we could have easily included as part of our donor research checking the parish website where we would have likely discovered they were kicking off a campaign—and even that our potential major donors were heading up the effort. With this information, we would have modified our personal appeal to acknowledge and commend their parish commitment, revising our own "ask" to a lower amount with fulfillment beginning after their parish campaign concluded.

Our second rejection came from a man whose wife, unbeknown to our office, had died of cancer six months earlier. In addressing our initial communications to both him and his wife, we revealed to the prospect that we truly did not know much about him or his grief and personal burden. Unfortunately, asking for a donation was the office's first personal encounter with the prospect following his wife's death. We betrayed a certain insensitivity by failing to first offer any emotional support or even a sympathy card. The donor rejected our request for a campaign gift.

Remind volunteers and staff about the importance of communicating with development the important life changes in donors' lives.

We might want to believe no one was to blame. Yet since our Vincentian members knew the family personally, had our own internal communications been more thorough, the development office and the provincial one would have known of the wife's illness and reached out sooner. This case illustrates the importance of keeping in frequent contact with donors and the potential personal hurt (and financial loss) that can ensue when that contact lapses.

Remind employees, volunteers, community members, and staff frequently about the importance of communicating with the development department regarding important life changes in donors' lives (deaths, illness, anniversaries, birthdays, awards, and so on). As development officers, we do well to make sure we are aware of which members or officers in the organization maintain the most frequent contact with the donor. Prior to making a major "ask," check sources for relevant information. In this example, having done this would have averted embarrassment and hurt. We also would have deferred our appeal and concentrated instead on the higher priority—ministering to this man's immediate emotional and spiritual needs.

Repairing Hurt Feelings

Let us nurture deep and fulfilling friendships based on mutual trust, humility, gratitude, Christian love, and our common desire to serve the mission. What is it that makes one trustworthy? In Vincent's words: "One does not believe a man because he is learned but because he seems to be a good man and because we love him" (Pujo, p. 113).

When one national membership organization's new executive director took over in 2000, he heard about a generous local chapter donor and volunteer who for years had seemed indifferent, even hostile, toward the national organization. The director learned that some two decades earlier, the donor's local chapter had nearly closed because of what was later recognized to be an ill-conceived policy implemented by several powerful members on the national board.

The new director flew out to meet the donor in person. He reminded the donor that the people with whom he was angry had all left the organization. The director assured the donor that current leaders supported success for all local chapters and was certainly not in the business of shutting chapters down.

The donor was convinced. In the decade since, he has given $500+ annually and recently joined the organization's top 100 lifetime donors.

"People make decisions, not the organization," the director reminds us. "I've rebuilt damaged relationships by helping donors find a way to not throw the baby out with the bath water. They may be angry with one or more people, but they can usually find a way to successfully continue supporting the charity's mission."

Asking for Too Much

Fundraisers hear early and often in their training, "If their mouths don't fall open when you ask for the gift, you didn't ask for enough." This is not always true.

Some time ago, I began the typical research to identify a donor to underwrite a considerable expense for our capital campaign kick-off dinner. I reviewed one prospect's giving history to the Vincentians and other charities. When research uncovered a $50,000 donation he had made to his parish's renovation campaign, I determined, along with other factors, an appropriate "ask" to be $25,000. I was only asking for half because I reasoned the Vincentians probably were more removed from his daily life than his own parish where he receives the sacraments and is personally involved.

The donor's mouth did not drop open in awe; he laughed out loud. He explained he had no means to contribute anywhere near that figure. Furthermore, only once before had he been able to make a large contribution—two years prior when he had allocated money from his sister's bequest for the parish to which they both belonged.

Had I been more patient and less quick to make so large an "ask," our conversation might have revealed this important fact in due course, saving us both some uncomfortable moments. The lessons of impatience and immoderation are age-old; Vincent de Paul himself wrestled with these issues. Often he found himself reining in the unbridled enthusiasm of friends and co-workers who rushed into ill-conceived projects only to see their efforts come to nothing. "I see nothing more frequently than the failure of things undertaken in haste," he observed (Pujo, p. 119).

Inasmuch as the donor's openness suggested a willingness to continue the conversation, I thanked him for everything he had already done for the Vincentians and for the modest pledge he was able to make. As he admitted wanting to participate in a much bigger way, over the course of the next month we kept in touch. I met him a second, and even a third time, discussing how he might help us organize some volunteers for this major undertaking. He agreed to call some key business contacts he knew from among our vendors; his efforts ultimately led to a gift-in-kind worth $10,000. This collaboration moved us well beyond rejection, giving our donor a deep sense of fulfillment.

"We have to be careful that the person does not need the money more than we do."

The experience itself is a worthy lesson. I no longer assume every major giver has personal wealth. The most compelling advice on fundraising are wise words from a former executive of the Sisters of St. Joseph of Carondelet, Sister Mary Ann Nestel. "We have to be careful," she warned, "that the person from whom we're asking a gift does not need the money more than we do."

In short, do not ask too soon. But don't give up too soon, either! Even when a willing prospect's financial situation precludes a significant donation, persistence can lead to any number of meaningful ways in which they can contribute significantly without opening their checkbook.

Steady, Generous Donor Wants Out

Nothing is quite as devastating as a major donor asking to be removed from future solicitations. When this happened recently in our office, we moved quickly to find out why. We had no inkling the donor was unhappy or had been offended. She was well acquainted with our work and knew many of the community members. She even sent her customary annual appeal gift when making her request.

We made it a top priority to discover her reasons for rejecting future solicitations. In addition to the formal, personalized thank-you letter the head of the organization always sends, we also mailed a handwritten note thanking her for her donation and letting her know we would honor her request. We also included a prayer card enrolling her in the Vincentians' prayer ministry program in gratitude for her faithful support of the mission. We invited her to share special intentions for our members to include in prayer. Finally, we asked if there was any other way the Vincentians might assist her at this time.

We were resolute in responding with gratitude—and more personalization.

We did all this in writing because in this case, phone calls were not appropriate. We wrote that we were happy to continue sending her newsletters to keep her apprised of our work. (All newsletters include a return envelope.) Two months later we mailed her the latest newsletter, including a special envelope with a personal note updating her on one of our community members whom she knows very well. We did not give up. One month later we mailed an Easter card. Eight weeks later, we sent another newsletter with a personal message from one of our members.

This time, the donor sent a gift. We never did learn why she asked to be removed from future solicitations. We were resolute, however, in responding with continuing gratitude—and even more personalization.

Most donors are bombarded with solicitations from dozens of charities as well as personal requests from their children, grandchildren, neighbors, parishioners, schools, and others. We now take time to find new ways to help our best donors know they are important to us and that we are thinking of them.

One idea we use is calling one donor per day, just to say thank you and share good news about the people we serve. It takes only two to three minutes. We absolutely look forward to that call. It is rewarding and most enjoyable.

Consider two more ways to thank big donors, with the focus on what comprises a meaningful gesture in the donor's mind (and not what is more efficient or easier for your organization). Pretend you are the major donor being thanked. Which of the following gestures of gratitude would mean more to you personally? Which would surprise you more?

1. You receive an email invitation to a private breakfast and tour being held on an upcoming Friday morning exclusively for the charity's VIP contributors.

2. You answer your doorbell to find a representative of the charity with a bag of home-baked cookies and a cheerful word of thanks for you.

Special events for big donors are common. Delivering cookies may in the end take no more time or resources, and imagine the singular impact such a simple gesture might make.

Showing gratitude and taking a personal interest in supporters is one of the best ways to avert rejection.

Recently a friend told me her pastor came to watch her son and another parishioner perform in their high school play. A week later, her son received a handwritten note in the mail from the pastor congratulating him on his effort. Mind you, this is not a rural parish serving a couple hundred people—more than 2,000 families belong to this church. What's more, parishioners routinely see their pastor riding his bike through the neighborhoods and subdivisions, knocking on parishioners' doors just to say hello and ask how everything is going.

Showing gratitude and taking a personal interest in members and supporters is one of the best ways to avert the rejection that comes when constituents lose a feeling of unity with the organization's people and mission.

Maybe donor relationships need more cookies at the front door and fewer VIP receptions. Maybe we fundraisers should be more like the pastor who cares for his flock in such a personal way and less like employees primarily worried about the proverbial bottom line. Are we too busy doing what is urgent while neglecting what is important? It is far easier to keep an existing donor than to acquire a new one.

Addressing Donor Attrition

Lapsing donors are a charity's perennial concern. Whereas major donors warrant more time and personalized attention, similar efforts to learn a low-level donor's reason for lapsing are usually not possible. However, sending a survey instead of an appeal to longer lapsed contributors can provide valuable information.

Construct a questionnaire that encourages honest feedback about the reason for lapsing. This gives the donor a chance to air grievances or otherwise "excuse" themselves from your base of contributors. Offering preprinted choices will help relieve potential guilty feelings the donor may have about writing out the answer.

Your survey might go something like this:

As a member of [the organization's] extended family, you have shared generously in our mission to [list primary mission]. Please take a few moments to help us understand your relationship with and insights about our organization.

(1) In what way(s) have you been involved with [the organization]?

[ ] As a volunteer or member

[ ] I know or am related to a member

[ ] As a past donor

[ ] As a board member

[ ] Other: _____

(2) If you have contributed financially to [the organization] in the past but have not recently, please tell us why:

[ ] I have lost touch with [the organization's] mission.

[ ] I have redirected my support to other charitable causes.

[ ] I do not have enough information about how my contributions are used.

[ ] Changes in my income mean I am no longer able to contribute.

[ ] I support the organization in other ways, such as:

Comments, questions and concerns: _____

(3) Which activities would you be most likely to support in the future?

[ ] [list the organization's principle activities]

[ ]

[ ]

[ ]

[ ] Other: _____

(4) Kindly indicate your willingness to receive future updates and information about [the organization] and the people we are helping:

[ ] Yes, please keep me on your mailing list.

[ ] Please remove my name from appeals and solicitations, but send updates on your activities.

[ ] Please remove my name from all correspondence (greeting cards, newsletters, etc.)

(5) We are grateful for your support. If you would like to share specific thoughts or intentions, we would be happy to hear from you.

We all appreciate being asked our opinion since it shows respect for our personal beliefs and concerns. Of course, fundraisers always will include a return envelope for the potential next gift.

Recently I spoke with the executive of a men's college fraternity—which targeted an age-based direct-mail appeal to several thousand lapsed alumni donors—who attended college in the 1960s. Rather than highlight how the fraternity is achieving success today, its message and graphics reminisced about "your glory days in the brotherhood." The outer envelope and one colorful, fold-over insert featured a football theme with photos from the recipients' collegiate era. Language invited them to "remember the good ol' days" and "get back in the game." The piece succeeded in its goal to reconnect with long-lost donors on an emotional, not intellectual, level. Response was more than double that of the typical "lapsed letter" appeal, raising $20,000+ from 101 donors.

Be Not Afraid

Wrapping up a capital campaign, one community of Catholic priests and brothers was short of their goal by just $1,250. They decided to turn first to major donors who already had pledged and were thus vested in the outcome. The first donor declined the invitation to give an additional gift to close the campaign. However, the next donor said he was honored to be asked. What's more, he drove two hours to hand deliver the check that would take the campaign to its goal. The community created a plaque that gratefully recognized his family for their generosity.

We are doing more than asking for money; we are inviting others to join our mission.

Our lesson here? Have no fear! We are doing more than asking for money; we are inviting others to join our mission. In giving them an opportunity to do good with their resources, we are providing a way for them to take the next step of their own spiritual or benevolent journey.

Conclusion

The most seasoned professional fundraiser may correctly analyze and evaluate donor habits, diligently follow industry best practices, practice due diligence, effectively test, and study the donor base. Yet in the end this same professional readily will admit that any individual's "donor behavior" and giving pattern is almost wholly unpredictable.

Moving beyond rejection sometimes means accepting rejection as the best possible outcome. Such an understanding is foolishness by professional standards. Yet, it is not only possible but advisable for benevolent organizations. Charitable work carries within it the wisdom to value goodness over success, the long-term outcome over the short-term, and the truth that what this world treasures most usually means little or nothing when you're thinking spiritually.

It is a lesson Vincent de Paul learned time and again. In calmly accepting the Congregation's failure to establish itself in Hibernia despite valiant missionary efforts spanning six years, Vincent announced confidently, "It is enough for God to know the good which has been done here" (Pujo, p. 168).

When fundraisers focus more on results than on fidelity to the mission, frustration and weariness undoubtedly set in. To guard against such a mindset, we can again look to Vincent's own wise counsel:

> Vincent continued to move forward only to the extent that the needs he saw could be supported by the means at his disposal. It seems that for a long time, he was torn between the desire to respond to every appeal of the poor . . . and his economic prudence which kept him from throwing himself into distant ventures. He wrote to Bernard Codoing, who was always ready to undertake new projects: "The works of God are not accomplished in this way; they carry themselves out, and those works which God does not support soon die. Let us move slowly toward our ambitions." (Pujo, p. 160.)

In patience and perseverance, then, let us measure our success by faithfulness before fruitfulness.

Two stories illustrate this point, a happy conclusion to rest any notion that we on our own have accomplished anything at all.

A few months into the capital campaign to build a residence for senior Vincentian priests and brothers, one of the priests asked me to dinner with him and his close friend who was visiting from out of town. The friend had attended Kenrick-Glennon Seminary in St. Louis and was taught by the Vincentians. Clearly this was to be a social visit and not a solicitation meeting. Inasmuch as I grew up in St. Louis, we chatted at lunch about people and places we knew in common. During the course of our conversation, the priest mentioned our excitement over plans to build the new home. To my utter amazement, his friend announced he would certainly like to support such a worthy project. Then he proceeded to commit to a $50,000 pledge for the capital campaign. Making an "ask" had not even been on my agenda—yet, as Vincent would have said, "God revealed again the graciousness of divine Providence" for our needs.

The last story comes to us from the executive director of two Missouri children's homes who was to give a talk to members of a small, rural congregation. On the appointed Sunday, Bob made the three-and-a-half hour drive, anticipating how the crowd might respond to his address about the agency's work. Arriving at the church, Bob's hopes fell. He would be speaking to no more than a couple dozen churchgoers sparsely dotting the pews. *Certainly a waste of time,* he thought. Yet by the day's end Bob realized his judgment was based on human wisdom. Once again, "divine Providence" prevailed in the actions of one elderly woman. After hearing about the agency's mission, she told Bob she intended to name the organization as a beneficiary in her will. Two years later the children's home received that legacy—a $1 million bequest.

Let us therefore take up each day's work, mindful of lessons from the field, accepting success and rejection not as a measure of our own worth as fundraisers, but as means to draw us closer to our mission. May we value steadfastness over success, practicing at every moment patience, perseverance, gratitude, humility, and genuine concern for the donor.

Questions for Discussion

1. Vincent was quite likeable—he asked, people gave. How likeable is our organization? How do we develop personal relationships with our donors?

2. Rejection is part of our business. What are our organizational rejection stories? What can we learn from them? How do we deal with rejection?

3. People are attracted to organizational missions when their own personal values match up with the organizational values. How do we communicate our mission and values? How do we help our donors discover their own values and show how they match up to our mission?

9

Raising Awareness and Resources in Response to Homelessness

MARK MCGREEVY AND LIANNE HOWARD-DACE

Our vocation is to go, not just to one parish, not just to one diocese, but all over the world.
—Vincent de Paul

IN 1994 Princess Diana came to reopen newly refurbished Willesden Hostel for Depaul International, which co-ordinates the activities of Depaul charities operating in the UK, Ireland, Slovakia, Ukraine, France, and the United States. Depaul's services offer support to homeless and disadvantaged people of all ages; Willesden Hostel would operate for young homeless people in the north west of London.

Having Diana support us was both a tremendous privilege and, of course, an enormous fundraising opportunity for a relatively new charity. Depaul International had managed similar events in the seven years that Diana had been involved with us. However, nothing could prepare us for the insane media attention that followed her wherever she went. Everything had to be meticulously planned and stage managed from half an hour before she arrived until half an hour afterwards.

To that end, the Buckingham Palace press secretary had visited the site of the visit months before, along with Princess Diana's senior lady in waiting. Together we timetabled the three hours of the visit with stop-watch accuracy minute by minute. We were asked to write the speeches one month in advance and submit them to ensure no duplication and that the timings worked. We developed a press statement and agreed upon "sound bites," which would work in different media formats—radio, television, and (most importantly for us in relation to fundraising potential) the newspapers. With the visual images of the day being as important as the written word for the front page of newspapers, Diana also needed to consider what to wear. What were the colors of the charity logo? What would be the perfect place for the killer photograph to ensure we got the maximum publicity for the cause?

On the day of the event itself, the press arrived early. This was at the height of Diana-Mania. There were literally hundreds of press with journalists and photographers crowded behind barriers in addition to camera crews for numerous countries. Add to that the thousands of well-wishers, and the excitement was palpable.

Diana arrived on time with a big convoy of police and palace officials. As usual she looked stunning. It was a hot day so she was understandably wearing a very short dress, but as agreed the colors worked well with the logo of the charity. As soon as she stepped out of the car the paparazzi went mad. Cameras flashed for about ten minutes as Diana patiently posed for them next to our charity banner. After everyone got the shots they wanted, we went inside and the event unfolded perfectly as planned. The departure attracted a similar feeding frenzy, but Diana was again brilliant and patient before departing for home.

All of us involved in the organization of the event were delighted. We knew we were a front page story across the world and that could only raise our profile, which in turn should bring in some much needed donations—a success all round!

The next morning everyone at central office got up early and waited for the newspapers to be delivered. As expected we were the front page on every edition (and indeed across the world). However, the headline was not "Diana and the Homeless" or "Diana and Depaul" as we had hoped. In nine out of ten papers, the headline was "Princess Thigh-ana" or "Princess Raises Temperatures." The newspapers had clearly focused on the mixture of a sunny spell of weather in the UK and Diana in a short skirt to promote a feel good glamorous upbeat image in keeping with the mood of the nation. The charity banner was cropped out of the shot altogether, and most papers didn't even mention she had been visiting a charity—let alone that the charity was called Depaul. From a fundraising point of view, it was a disaster. We had been the center of the media world for one day, yet we didn't gain one additional supporter. A model lesson in how not to use a fundraising opportunity.

> *Everyone involved learned some valuable lessons about scenario planning, setting achievable outcomes, and the importance of reflecting on the experience to ensure our fundraising is as good as it can be.*

Diana was, needless to say, very disappointed, but there was no blame on her part. Other events she hosted both before and after raised enormous amounts for Depaul and for other causes she was passionate about. The truth is even though she tried her hardest on this occasion, sometimes fundraising is more about "serendipity" than the science some people claim. However, that said, everyone involved learned some valuable lessons about scenario planning, setting achievable outcomes, and the importance of constantly reflecting on the experience of our own efforts and that of others to ensure our fundraising is as good as it can be. We owe that much to the people we serve, even if we sometimes don't live up to expectations because of events outside of our control.

What follows is a snapshot of some of Depaul's experiences of fund-raising and advocacy. There is no guarantee of success, but it may elicit further ideas and creativity.

Vision and Values

Vincent de Paul is the Patron Saint of Charity. Like charities the world over, he represents a bridge between the rich and the poor, the powerful and the powerless, charity and justice. His Congregation of the Mission and the Daughters of Charity worked directly with those in need, but he also facilitated ways for other people to be involved in this work, whether through active participation or through donations to provide services to the poor.

The personal Vincentian call to action ("Something must be done; what am I—or we or you—going to do?") and the desire to work in collaboration with others have inspired many movements and charitable organizations over the centuries. It is an inspiring vision. In delivering on that vision, Vincent developed a very strong and enduring set of values and behaviors. Depaul International and its subsidiaries are just the latest incarnation of that Vincentian vision.

"Something must be done; what am I—or we or you— going to do?"

Depaul UK was the first of Depaul International's group of charities. It was formed in 1989 at the initiative of the late Cardinal Basil Hume, who brought together the Daughters of Charity, the St. Vincent de Paul Society, and the Passage Day Centre (another Vincentian-led project) to set up a new organization to respond to the needs of growing numbers of vulnerable young people living and sleeping on the streets of London. Within ten years Depaul UK had grown nationally to become the largest provider of services to homeless young people. It specialized in working with marginalized groups such as active homeless drug users, those with alcohol problems, and ex-offenders. These groups were neglected by state agencies and existing charities at that time but were seen by trustees and staff at Depaul UK as the modern day "poorest of the poor." That was to set a benchmark for how the charity would develop.

As a result of its growing reputation in the UK, in 2001 the Irish government invited Depaul to establish services in Ireland, working with similar marginalized groups of all ages. Depaul Ireland quickly grew and is now the largest of the Depaul subsidiaries, working in both the North and South of the country and respected by both Catholic and Protestant communities for the inclusiveness of its projects.

Following the success of this first move out of the UK and in consultation with the Vincentian Family, Depaul International was formed in 2004 with the ambitious aim of gradually growing its capacity over time to tackle homelessness at a global level. It acts as a parent company for the subsidiaries in different countries and has three roles:

- To support and co-ordinate work in existing charities (including fundraising)
- To ensure our Vincentian values are put into practice through the formation of trustees, staff and volunteers
- To develop new subsidiaries in partnership with the Vincentian Family (again, includes fundraising)

In 2006 Depaul Slovensko opened in Bratislava, Slovakia, providing a night shelter and infirmary for the homeless, and Depaul Kharkiv opened in Ukraine in 2007, providing street outreach services and medical support for children sleeping in the underground sewers and heating vents of the city. Depaul USA opened in 2009 in Philadelphia, Pennsylvania, providing transitional housing for men leaving the shelter program, and the Daybreak center recently opened in Macon, Georgia, providing services for homeless men and women. Depaul has over 75 projects working with over 13,000 homeless people every year. It has over 600 full-time staff and a similar number of volunteers.

In the last twenty-three years, Depaul has grown from a $300,000 per annum charity to one that raises $30,000,000 per annum today. That has involved some good fortune, but it is due for the most part to hard work in developing the right strategies and structures to achieve our financial goals. It is rooted in the wise words of Sr. Vincent Murray, a Daughter of Charity in the UK, who volunteered in our fundraising department in the formative years of the charity. She advised us to adopt an old Russian fisherman's motto: "Pray to God, but row for the shore." In other words, have faith, but put in the work!

"Pray to God, but row for the shore."

If you looked at the journey of Depaul through the theoretical lens of organizational development, it has been a tremendous success—a strong sense of values-driven vision and mission, with committed staff and volunteers, year-on-year growth, and the capacity to respond to new and emerging needs. However, maintaining fundraising momentum is a problem at any time, for any charity, of any size. This is especially true at this time of global financial crisis, when more people than ever need our services but there is less money to spend.

So how is Depaul consolidating its $30 million current target? How is it planning to grow to meet new needs? How do agencies make sure that homeless and marginalized people get what they need? How do agencies make people aware and sympathetic to the problem of homelessness in all its different forms and geographic locations? How do agencies convince governments and other potential donors to be part of the answer to that problem?

Learning from the Past

Raising awareness and securing funding is an integral part of any work to serve the poor. With all the will in the world, it is not possible to tackle the issues of poverty and injustice without the necessary resources, as records of Vincent's work show us. There really is "nothing new under the sun" (Ecclesiastics 1:9).

Vincent himself faced many of the same funding challenges as contemporary charities in ensuring a diverse income mix and balancing restricted and unrestricted funds. Vincent, like Depaul International, raised money from government sources (the French Royal Court), individual donors (both small and large amounts), foundations and businesses, events and endowments, and, importantly, through the Church and associated communities.

The following sections will reflect on some examples of how Depaul International has raised money in these different areas and what we have learned as a result. All of this is interspersed with a few anecdotes about Vincent himself, who was somewhat of a master of modern fundraising techniques before it became a profession in its own right.

The Power of Story

Fundamentally we must always remember that fundraising is at the same time a science and an art form. With modern research, marketing methods, and intelligent in-house databases, large charities can predict with some measure of certainty what they will get in return for an investment in a particular campaign. Let's say they want to raise $100,000 by attracting an average gift of $50 per person. The charity would profile the kind of individual they are targeting and the income bracket that individual would need to have to give that much. They would use the data they might already have or buy donor lists of people who might have supported previous campaigns. The charity would then develop a storyline that would speak directly to the targeted individual. It may be a story of a disaster that has already happened. It may be a forecast disaster that could be prevented. It might be a celebration of success because of an action already taken and an encouragement to do more.

In any case, the science side of fundraising will have a target it expects to reach and a methodology to get you there.

Good senior fundraisers will tell you that they spend 80 percent of their time telling or writing stories.

However, as important as the science is, it will only work if there is a powerful story to tell. The campaign will only speak to people if it genuinely shines a strong light on the cause it is promoting and on the mission of the charity itself and the values it upholds. That is why people give—not because the science behind a campaign draws a logical conclusion. Charities that can't tell their story effectively will fail over time.

Good senior fundraisers will tell you that they spend 80 percent of their time telling or writing stories. How many charities fail within years after their founder moves on? It's because the story of the organization isn't owned by enough people and therefore gradually fades. At Depaul, everybody hears the story of the organization at induction and every opportunity is taken to revisit that story or to get staff to tell their own story of life within Depaul. In that sense everyone is a fundraiser. This oral history evolves over time, and it is important that somebody takes the responsibility to write it down, update it, and celebrate it. Anniversaries, speeches when long-serving staff leave, staff conferences—these are all a time to celebrate the power of story and keep it alive in the organization.

The King's Shilling

For many years Depaul UK provided services with very little money coming from government sources. In the 1990s the crisis of street homelessness grew to epidemic proportions as a result of policy changes—especially in the big cities. We, along with other agencies involved in homelessness, began to lobby strongly for change. We took politicians from across the political divide out onto the streets at night, invited them into shelters, ran press campaigns, and encouraged celebrities to raise awareness of the issue. In this regard Princess Diana was a close friend to Depaul and particularly effective as documented previously. However, we also owe our thanks to countless other celebrities who took time to learn about and promote our cause, including journalists and sports personalities. In particular, Cherie Blair (wife of Tony Blair) was a speaker at several events for Depaul. While she had no influence on the political decision making, she did help us to articulate our case in a way that politicians can understand.

After months, perhaps a year, of chipping away at the issue with the help of others, the homeless sector managed to swing public opinion such that street homelessness became an election issue to which politicians had to respond. As a result, hundreds of millions of government pounds were made available to resolve street homelessness once and for all. A unit was set up within central government to co-ordinate the effort. It was a great victory, but it was exactly at that point that some homeless agencies began to have their doubts about where that victory might actually lead.

The phrase "the King's shilling" comes from the First World War when conscripts were given a small payment for signing up to fight on the Western Front. In return for a shilling, you signed a form. From that moment on, you did exactly what you were told even if you didn't like it. For some charities, funding from central government presented the same dilemma—would taking large amounts of money from government affect the sector's ability to advocate or criticize? Would hiring lots of professional full-time staff dilute the vocational element in organizations that had previously relied on volunteers?

These were, and continue to be, good questions. Each agency must be sure they have thought through the implications for themselves. However, from Depaul's point of view, it seemed churlish to have lobbied government for more resources and to then refuse to help in delivering them. Who better than Depaul to ensure they would be targeted effectively at those who had the most desperate needs? A partnership with government can be educational to both parties. It is possible (as we have found) to work in partnership but maintain the organization's integrity to speak out against injustice. From Depaul's experience, working with central, local, or city authorities has been essential to our success. It has given us a good platform for dialogue with politicians and civil servants, but it has also greatly helped us in providing a secure base of income in many of the countries in which we work.

A partnership with government can be educational to both parties.

For Depaul, co-operation with government around working with the most marginalized is at the heart of building a civil society. If we set about it in the right way, it can only help lead to the structural change that the Vincentian family promotes globally.

Individual Donors Large and Small

Individual giving makes up a significant portion of funding for charities in the Depaul group and varies greatly—from someone who anonymously puts a coin in a collecting bucket on the street to those who give large sums of money and may have programs or buildings named in their honor. The key to successful fundraising from individuals is to remember exactly that—they are individuals, and each will have different motivations, expectations, and capacities to give.

Individual giving is all about building and managing relationships to keep people engaged with your cause. Vincent knew this and was able to build relationships with people from all walks of life with different abilities to give. He engaged with his supporters through his letters, talking about his work and its recent developments and explaining the need that their funds would help address.

Vincent understood that to be moved to give, people must understand the need. We know that he took some of the Ladies of Charity to see the people he was working with firsthand in order to encourage them further. "The first thing he did was to invite the Ladies of Charity to visit the Couche [foundling hospital]. His reason for doing this was not so much to let them see the evil as to encourage them to suggest a remedy" (Roman, p. 487).

Vincent understood that to be moved to give, people must understand the need.

Today nonprofits use an increasing variety of means—images, videos, as well as the written word—to similarly connect their donors with the work of their organization. The tools that are available to us may have evolved, but the principles of relationship building are the same as they were in Vincent's time.

Depaul has been fortunate to have developed relationships with a number of high-value donors over the years who have made significant contributions to our work. Much has been written about the importance of trustee networks, research, and cultivation events. While these are important (the science), it will come to nothing unless a meaningful relationship develops. Sometimes that might be because of a shared faith perspective. Often it is because the cause resonates with an experience within their own family. Wealth does not shield people from mental illness or addiction.

It is important, if someone does show an interest, not to race to the finish line as fast as possible. The aim is to build a relationship based on mutual respect, not just secure a one-off donation and set people adrift. At Depaul, we spend a lot of time taking people to see our projects. We want them to understand what we do and what our mission is and to allow people to contribute their ideas as to how we build the charity. It can take two or three years with a significant donor for the first donation to arrive, but it is usually the case that the gift is ongoing, rather than one-time.

It can take two or three years with a significant donor for the first donation to arrive.

Of course, not everyone is able to make large gifts, but small gifts can also add up to have a significant impact on a charity's work. We may be reminded of the story in the Bible in which Jesus praised the widow woman in the temple who gave two small copper coins—not much to some, but to her it was a great deal of money (Luke 21:1–4). "The widow's mite" is the bedrock of most charities, and it tends to be the income stream that holds up best both in times of growth and recession.

Volunteer fundraisers can play an important role in the solicitation of small value gifts, from holding a street collection to organizing events in their community and gaining sponsorship for undertaking various challenges. With careful stewardship, the relationship with donors of small-value gifts can be developed so that they engage further with the cause and choose to give larger amounts or with greater frequency.

iHobo

The development of new technologies has huge potential to help charities grow their networks and reach new audiences, as well as offering new mechanisms for giving. A highly innovative way in which Depaul UK has raised funds and awareness in recent years is through their iHobo iPhone application. With pro bono assistance from a long-term corporate supporter, the creative agency Publicis London, in May, 2010, Depaul UK launched one of the first, and to date most successful, charity apps in the world.

iHobo is a live action game that puts a young homeless man on your phone for three days. During this time users have to answer alerts, including some in the middle of the night, and make decisions about what to give the young man to help him most. If you are there for iHobo and give him the right things, such as a sleeping bag and food, he can survive life on the streets and seek the help he needs. But if you ignore his alerts and give him the wrong things, his life spirals out of control and he may use the money you give him to buy drugs or resort to criminal activity.

The app included many ground-breaking uses of technology, including live action, multiple push notifications, and integrated use of text donations. This, along with the intentionally provocative nature of the app's name, caught the attention of the global press. The app has been a resounding success for Depaul UK. Downloaded over 600,000 times, iHobo has generated significant small one-off donations and grown Depaul UK's email marketing database by over 5,000 contacts. Staff from the UK have been asked to speak about iHobo at a number of conferences, which, coupled with the press attention around the app, has opened a number of doors for the corporate fundraising team, driving around $170,000 of corporate support.

"We should be innovative unto infinity."

Vincent de Paul commented that "we should be innovative unto infinity." Innovation can produce tension—particularly in the world of new media where stories can spiral out of control on Twitter and Facebook. iHobo wasn't without its share of controversy. But having consulted with a group of young service beneficiaries about the app's name and content, Depaul UK was confident that it was a risk worth taking. It has really paid off. Depaul UK is now looking for ways to develop the relationships with the donors who have given through the app, including using the phone numbers garnered from the text donations to have conversations and encourage them to commit to a regular gift.

Foundations and Corporate Support

Foundations can prove to be a significant income stream for charities. They are set up by individuals, families, and organizations who are passionate about philanthropy and may be more open to funding difficult work than the general population. Most foundations have a specific remit in which they choose to focus their giving, which allows organizations to write targeted applications to the ones that they know support their type of work. Depaul enjoys relationships with a number of foundations that provide funding for its programs in different countries. For example, in Ukraine where we work with street children, Mary's Meals (a Scottish charitable foundation) pays for the food costs for our street outreach service and our day center, ensuring that each child gets a nutritious meal each day. However, it is another foundation altogether that provides the medical care for what we do there. In looking at a developing service, we find it best to break down the project into smaller packages. That way, if somebody wants to, or can only afford to, fund part of what we do, they have the opportunity to do so.

Corporate fundraising is about relationship building.

Corporate giving can come in a variety of forms; some organizations will give cash donations, others will donate gifts-in-kind or provide pro-bono staff support in their area of expertise. Some corporations may even partner with a charity to launch and support new programs of work. Remember, a business is a group of people. Through influential staff within a company, corporate fundraising is as much about relationship building as are other types of fundraising.

Depaul UK has a variety of significant partnerships with corporate supporters. Over several years, we have developed a strong bond with the CEO of a British toy company that owns the rights to the Rubik's Cube. As well as their regular annual gift, in 2010 a specially made Rubik's Cube with each side representing a different aspect of Depaul UK's work was produced, and a large number of them gifted to Depaul. The community fundraising team has been able to use these at events to engage with potential individual supporters; the instantly recognizable cube is a great way to catch people's attention, and the fact that it can seem difficult to put right without the right knowledge is a great metaphor for the complexity of youth homelessness.

As well as cash donations, this relationship has given Depaul UK tools and opportunities with which to build its capacity to attract further support. In June 2011, a further dimension to the relationship developed; Rubik's sponsored a world record attempt for the most people solving the Rubik's Cube, donating $150 for each of the 300 people who took part.

As this example shows, corporate relationships can be multifaceted and organizations and businesses can discover different things they have to offer each other.

Events

Events can have many aims: they can be about building awareness, they can be a celebration with existing donors and stakeholders, they can be purely about raising money. An event strategy needs to clearly identify the purpose at the very outset. One thing for certain is that events are extremely time consuming. Depaul has run many events over the years—from receptions in the Houses of Parliament aimed at influencing politicians and policy makers, to a Mass at Westminster Cathedral for our committed supporters, staff, and volunteers. Both paid untold dividends. However, using events to raise money directly needs very careful thought. Without a dedicated public relations team, it is not something we would advise to any small- or medium-sized charity. In our experience what works best is setting up ad hoc event committees of committed and connected volunteers.

On one occasion some years ago, one of our trustees happened to know someone in the corporate world who could deliver us a private view of the Picasso Exhibition at the National Gallery in London. This gift meant that Depaul had no venue cost and that any monies raised would go directly to our projects around the world. With the help of a small group of women volunteers who were equally passionate about the work of Depaul, a ticket price was agreed upon, and, using their networks, the event quickly sold out. The same group managed to twist some arms and get discounted donations from catering and drinks companies and even used some of their musical sons and daughters to form a small string quartet to welcome the guests on arrival. Central office staff from Depaul did very little apart from provide information about the charity, which left them free to concentrate on other fundraising objectives. The volunteers enjoyed the event, and because there were no costs involved, the charity raised $75,000 for its projects.

Vincent de Paul understood the power of delegating event fundraising to people who shared his mission. For some of us, working with the poor face-to-face comes easily, for others helping to raise money is the gift that they bring. Vincent's Ladies of Charity are an early example of volunteer fundraisers.

Like the Ladies of Charity, we try to inspire people to be volunteer fundraisers on our behalf and help facilitate our mission. As well as donating money, some people throw themselves into fundraising on our behalf. The creativity and dedication of our supporters never fail to amaze us. Over the years, people have undertaken all kinds of different fundraising activities for us.

Legacies and Endowments

If a charity spends time developing relationships with people, then that cause can almost become part of the family. When that happens, things tend to follow a natural path. When the time comes, it's likely the charity will be recognized in a will or a longer-term endowment.

Depaul has benefited greatly from legacies. In some cases families have continued to keep a relationship with the charity long after the original contact has passed away. Recently one of our Depaul trustees left a significant sum of money for development of staff and volunteers by allowing them to share experience and skills across the group. This allowed one of our staff to spend two months in Paris developing our new charity there. On another occasion, a member of staff from Ireland, who has a specialty in the design of daycare centers, visited Slovakia to help with the redesign of our services there. This particular trustee was passionate about staff and volunteer development and building a shared sense of belonging within the Depaul Group. His legacy is fulfilling exactly that purpose, and members of his family have continued to be supportive along the same lines.

Endowment funds are a new area for Depaul but will become an increasing priority in the coming years. There are some recurring costs that do not excite people to give; for example, the necessary management and administration of the charity is dull in comparison to the needs of a street child in Ukraine. However, without one, the other cannot function. If management and administrative costs could be met, at least in part, by endowment funds provided by individuals who understand and appreciate the functions involved, this in turn allows more donated income to go directly to the real work of the charity.

Church and Community

From the beginnings of Depaul in the UK, Church and community donors have played an important role in funding our services. Our heritage from the Roman Catholic Church remains an important connection, and congregations across the countries where we work support our projects in a number of ways.

Parishes may dedicate a service especially to reflect on the needs of the homeless and the work of Depaul, remembering us in their prayers and holding a collection for our work. They may also collect items for us such as toiletries, which can be given to our beneficiaries. We support the churches that help us this way by producing materials they can use in their services, such as liturgical resources and educational activities for children. These are often linked to a specific seasonal appeal such as Lent or Advent and have proven to be a successful way for us to engage with churches across a wide area. Other community groups, both cross-denominational and secular, also support our work in a variety of ways.

Fundraising from communities is all about inspiring people to believe in your cause and mobilizing them to raise funds on your behalf. This brings together lots of small donations through various activities (such as bake sales) and is as much about friend-raising as it is about fundraising.

We are indebted to the many hundreds of volunteer champions who, having felt an affinity with our work, organize and solicit on our behalf within their own communities. These volunteers become advocates for our work and help raise funds from new audiences on a scale that our professional fundraisers simply could not achieve alone.

Conclusion

In relation to fundraising, little has changed since the days of Vincent de Paul. Like Depaul, Vincent received monies from the state, from individual donors, from businesses and foundations, from events, from legacies, from endowments, and from church and community.

Some of the processes might have become more sophisticated over time with Internet giving and social media, television and advertising. However, in his day Vincent himself showed "innovation unto infinity." He understood, as does Depaul, that sustainability is dependent on a mixed bag of funding sources and a network of dedicated staff and volunteers.

For all of the modern-day processes and management systems, fundraising will only be successful if it tells the story of who it is trying to serve in a sympathetic and compelling way. As charities we are promoting a particular cause to the world, and we have a duty to do that as well as we can and to gain as much support as we can. A central part of the Vincentian call to action is that we connect the rich with the poor, the haves with the have-nots, the powerful with the powerless, and we have a shared sense of charity leading to justice. Fundraising is one of the ways in which we do that.

Questions for Discussion

1. Vincent gave us the mandate to "be inventive to infinity." How are we creative in our organization? How often do we spend time exploring new ideas? What are the results?

2. In his best seller, *Good to Great,* Jim Collins told us to create BHAGs—"big, hairy, audacious goals." Does our organization set BHAGs for ourselves? Do I set BHAGs for myself?

3. Like Vincent's international expansion, Depaul grew from a few London-based homeless services to six countries in a few years. What can our organization learn from Depaul's methods for expansion?

10
Funding by Financing

J. Patrick Murphy, C.M.

*We have to borrow money to feed ourselves and for the assistance
relief of the poor country people who are waiting for us.*
—Vincent de Paul

WHILE VINCENT DE PAUL used his "outstanding ability to create
friendships" to raise the funds he needed, even his most eloquent
personal appeals had limits. When the King of France tired of Vincent's
persistently asking for funds for the poor, his frustration likely led to
the invention of the first public-private partnership. He gave Vincent an
international transportation company, the coaches of Soisson, and told
him to use the profits for his poor.

> With the age-old instinct of a peasant, [Vincent] gave priority to
> the possession of land and buildings, but like a knowing financier, he
> diversified the sources of his revenues, cultivating income from direct
> and indirect duties or from transport companies. (Pujo, p. 108.)

Like Vincent's example before us, effective modern institutions must
find ways to generate income from conducting business and diverting
profits to the nonprofit.

The Internal Revenue Service typically, if inadvertently, drives strategies for fundraising in the United States. Nonprofit organizations such

as colleges and universities receive tax-exempt status under section 501(c) 3 of the tax code. Under the IRS code, in general, universities can rent or lease investment property without tax risk if the entity rented is truly an investment. They can also own enterprises that fit within their tax-exempt status, such as a hospital for medical schools, cemeteries for alumni, golf courses, theaters, even airports.

As nonprofits develop alternative fundraising strategies and undertake projects to support their charitable purpose, they have to be mindful that IRS regulations may obligate the nonprofit to pay unrelated business income tax (UBIT). If, like Vincent's transportation company, the venture creates a revenue stream from operations, UBITs may well be worth paying.

Lyon and Healy Building Project

Several years ago, DePaul University expanded its Chicago Loop Campus by acquiring the Lyon and Healy Building. DePaul financed the purchase with tax-exempt bonds. The university then leased portions of the first floor to a fast-food restaurant, as an anchor tenant, and other retailers at prevailing market rates. DePaul further extended its financing strategy by selling steam (for heat) to the restaurant and the for-profit companies from its own boilers and priced the steam to escalate with the cost of energy index over time.

The strategy was for the rental income to eventually retire the bond debt. In other words, one floor of for-profit use would pay for the nine floors dedicated to nonprofit academic purposes.

A nonprofit allied with a government agent and a for-profit entity in a three-way public-private partnership.

DePaul struck a partnership with the City of Chicago to issue tax-exempt bonds under the city's home-rule authority. It was the first such partnership between Chicago and a nonprofit educational organization. DePaul could have financed the deal through federal programs; that, however, would have limited for-profit use to 5 percent of the total space. The city allowed 10 percent—conveniently, one floor of the ten-story building.

In this example, a nonprofit (DePaul) allied with a government agent (the City of Chicago) and a for-profit entity (the restaurant) in a three-way public-private partnership. All parties benefitted, but the greatest beneficiaries were DePaul's students. They escaped the burden of paying off a mortgage through higher tuition charges. They also got a favorite lunch spot only an elevator ride away from class.

Student Housing Project

In another example of a beneficial partnership with the for-profit sector, DePaul University joined with a private developer to build a residence hall on its Lincoln Park Campus. Unable to fund the project on its own, DePaul provided the land, and the developer financed the construction. Because of high student demand for housing, DePaul could guarantee tenants who in turn provided a steady flow of rent to the developer. After a period of years DePaul will become the owner of the building free and clear. The strategy allowed DePaul to offer its students housing in tony Lincoln Park at a more affordable rate than otherwise possible.

> From the beginning of his apostolate, Vincent de Paul was a man of action, an organizer and manager. He did not throw himself into a venture in haphazard fashion. Rather, he decided on a program, defined a method, and made sure of acquiring the wherewithal for the project. (Pujo, p. 71.)

More Examples

Recognizing the value of its existing in-house centralized high-speed copiers and design staff, DePaul University created a for-profit company.

Chicago Printworks supplied copying and printing services to the public from a storefront shop on its Loop Campus.

In 1986 the commercial insurance market became constrained. In response, fifty-five universities raised a risk pool of $50 million to provide liability insurance to institutions of higher learning. In the process they spawned a new insurance company. Initially a for-profit stock company, it filled an important need while generating income for its university investors. Changes in legal regulations have since allowed the venture to morph into a mutual insurance company that today is the dominant provider of liability products for the college and university market, delivering financial protection and benefits to all of its customers.

Recently inspired by a visionary donor, Viterbo University and the La Crosse Community Theater formed a partnership to build a theater in La Crosse, Wisconsin. The Weber Center for the Performing Arts fills a need that neither organization could afford alone.

DePaul University, Roosevelt University, and Columbia College created an independent nonprofit organization to construct and manage an eighteen-story residence hall strategically located near each institution's Chicago Loop campuses.

Many universities create research parks and lease them to entrepreneurs. The parks also provide opportunities for faculty to conduct research or provide consulting services. Often products invented in these research facilities get spun off into companies. In most cases the universities retain patents on products or share them with the faculty members who created them. Faculty members at Catholic University used such an opportunity to create a way to dissolve nuclear waste. The process renders the materials safe from leaching and permits safe disposal. The university partnered with a private firm to develop the process for commercial use. Revenues from patent rights became a lucrative source of income for the university.

Universities are not alone in finding revenue streams outside of traditional fundraising strategies. The Art Institute of Chicago offers visitors their choice of two restaurants and a gift shop. Hospitals provide restaurants (one Chicago hospital opened five new restaurants recently).

At the same time, it is good to know when to terminate operations that do not work out.

> As an experienced manager, Vincent de Paul kept a careful eye on the flow of the various revenues of the Congregation. At the end of 1642, he noticed that the royalties for the coaches of Soissons were not coming in regularly, although they were being requested daily. Therefore he decided to relinquish them. (Pujo, p. 156.)

Nonprofit organizations frequently squeeze budgets to do more mission without more revenue. At the same time, they rarely look at opportunities to delete programs that are failing or are drifting away from the core mission. Vincent was inventive about expanding revenue sources and was unafraid to cease operations that were failing—and to move on to something else.

Urgency, compassion, and creativity drive us to new solutions for age-old funding challenges. Creating new revenue sources spreads the risk of revenue shortfalls around—following the adage of not putting all your eggs in one basket. Or as Vincent, the trailblazer for modern, diversified fundraising, would say, "The charity of Christ compels us."

Questions for Discussion

1. Has our organization looked at alternative sources of revenue? What programs or services could we offer that would complement our mission and increase resources?

2. In the DePaul University example in the chapter, the "fundraisers" were the financial team (primarily). Who on our team could help find new streams of revenue, besides the development officers? Who could find ways to stop doing things that are worn out?

3. How are we measuring programs to determine which are working and which are not? Are we prepared to make the hard-nosed evaluations to jettison the ineffective ones? What steps should we take to ensure we are not wasting our effort or resources?

11
Lessons for Leaders
Ignite, Act, Lead from Humility

Let's work, let's work, let's go to the assistance of the poor
country people who are waiting for us.
—Vincent de Paul

VINCENT DEDICATED his life to observing the conditions of the poor wherever he found them—in the streets, in prisons, on his doorstep—and asking the quintessential question: "Something must be done; what must I do?" It is a perfect question to start our endeavors. We offer it here as a good place to end.

Ignite Like a Great Fire

In one of his final talks, Vincent challenged his listeners to think big—not to go into one place but to go to the ends of the earth—to inflame the hearts of people, like a fire radiating from the sun (Pujo, p. 251). His own fire in the belly was still raging with love for the poor, and he worked hard to inspire others to carry on after him.

Action Is Our Entire Task

Vincent took for his motto *"Totum opus nostrum in operatione consistit* (Action is our entire task)" (Pujo, p. 251). Yes, he pondered, and sometimes wavered, but for the most part, he was a man of action. He reformed the clergy in France; he changed the way society viewed the poor and prisoners. He was groundbreaking in valuing the contribution of women and their role in bettering society.

Vincent assisted abandoned children, prisoners, victims of catastrophe, refugees, and housebound invalids. "In all these works he was a precursor, showing the way which is still followed today by institutions and governmental departments of social service" (Pujo, p. 251). He recognized the poor as his figurative lords and masters, considering himself unworthy of serving them.

Leadership Flows from Humility

In our organizations, we have only incomplete, unfinished people. Truly, that's the only kind of person there is. Vincent started with the same sort. Robert K. Greenleaf, author of *The Servant Leader,* reminds us that there are no perfect people, so we must work with the half-people we have. It is a good place to start—the only place. If we serve them well, Greenleaf wrote, they will achieve great things.

Vincent found ordinary people to do extraordinary work. He found greatness in the simple people he attracted to the work of serving the poor. He gathered ordinary people, in his humble way, and trained and inspired them to excel in service of the poor.

For Vincent it started with humility—a virtue he struggled with all his life. He learned that once he had his pride under control—as a humble person—he could then serve the poor with personal freedom. He passed that insight on to his followers.

Pope Francis agrees with Vincent. "He believes that authentic humility empowers leaders like no other leadership quality:

'If we can develop a truly humble attitude, we can change the world,' wrote Bergoglio before becoming pope" (Krames, p. 7).

Even ordinary people—Vincent's family—deserve good care. "Vincent was concerned that an excess of economy should not result in starving the family. 'I have heard from one of our houses that the poor food provided there is harmful both to bodies and to souls,' and he made it clear that it is wrong to 'sell the best wine and then serve the worst stuff, or to expose the community to miserly treatment'" (Pujo, p. 187).

Leadership means taking care of the service providers—the followers. We all need to celebrate small wins, recognize people for the good they do, make an excuse to have a party once in a while.

Leadership is about people—selecting people capable of greatness when led well, serving people, caring for them, and inspiring all to action—like a great fire. Vincent was not the first to figure this out, but he did it *par excellence*—to the extent that his countrymen called him *Pere de la Patrie*—Father of the Country. We take up the challenge. Something must be done; what will we do?

The authors have offered their ideas in this book not as a manual of the fundamentals of fundraising for professionals, but rather to provide encouragement through stories of how good people linked their hard work and creative efforts to inspiration from their patron, Vincent de Paul.

We want to hear your stories as well. Mail them to Vincent on Leadership: The Hay Project at: DePaul University, School of Public Service, One E. Jackson Blvd., Chicago, IL, 60604, or email them to: hayleadership@depaul.edu.

You may also want to follow this blog: www.vincentianfundraising.org.

You can find additional free inspirational and practical resources at these Vincentian-related sites: leadership.depaul.edu, vincentonleadership.org, famvin.org.

Bibliography

Coste, Pierre, *The Life and Works of Saint Vincent de Paul,* 3 vols., (Westminster, MD, 1952).

de Paul, Saint Vincent. Correspondence, Conferences, Documents. Translated from the 1924 edition of Pierre Coste, CM. [Conf. to CM in the text]

Feillet, Alphonse, "Un chapitre inédit de l'histoire de la Fronde," Revue de Paris, 33 (1 August 1856).

Féron, Alexandre, *La vie et les oeuvres de Ch. Maignart de Bernières (1616-1662); l'organisation de l'assistance publique a l'époque de la Fronde* (Rouen, 1930).

Grell, Ole Peter, and Cunningham, Andrew, "The Counter-Reformation and Welfare Provision in Southern Europe," in *Health Care and Poor Relief in Counter-Reformation Europe* (London, 1999).

Guichard, Joseph, Notes and documents; printed original in Bibliothèque de l'Arsenal, ms. 2565, n° 2, recueil de règlements de charité.

Joyaux, Simone P., "Survival at Stake? Be More Donor-Centric," *The Nonprofit Quarterly,* May 14, 2009).

Krames, Jeffrey A., *Lead with Humility: 12 Leadership Lessons from Pope Francis,* Amacom: New York, 2015.

Lyons manuscript. Source: Jeanine Garé Depaule, *Les Lazaristes au XVIIe siècle d'après le manuscrit 869 de la Bibliothèque Municipale de Lyon*. 2 vols. Mémoire de Maîtrise. Histoire Moderne, 1986, Université Lyon III. [Copy in ACMP.]

McHugh, Tim, *Hospital Politics in Seventeenth-Century France: The Crown, Urban Elites, and the Poor* (Aldershot, England, 2007).

Pujo, Bernard. *Vincent de Paul, the Trailblazer*. Notre Dame, IN, University of Notre Dame, 2003.

Padberg, C. and Hannefin, D., D.C. (1982) "Saint Vincent's First Foundation: The Ladies of Charity," *Vincentian Heritage Journal:* Vol. 3: Iss. 1, Article 3. Available at: http://via.library.depaul.edu/vhj/vol3/iss1/3.

Robineau, Louis, *Remarques sur les actes et paroles de feu Monsieur Vincent de Paul notre très Honoré Père et Fondateur*, ed. André Dodin (Paris, 1991), art. 302, p. 136.

Roman, C.M., Jose Maria, *St. Vincent DePaul: A Biography*, London: Melisende, 1999.

The Society of Saint Vincent de Paul National Council, *Manual* (Maryland Heights, Mo.; 2007). SVdPUSA Publisher.

The Society of Saint Vincent de Paul National Council, *Society of Saint Vincent de Paul Response to Hurricane Katrina: The Largest Disaster in U.S. History* [*Response to Katrina* in the text], (Maryland Heights, Mo.; 2007). SVdPUSA Publisher.

Contributors

PATRICIA M. BOMBARD, B.V.M., is director of Vincent on Leadership: The Hay Project and a part-time faculty member in DePaul University's School of Public Service. She teaches values-centered leadership in Chicago, abroad, and online. She holds a doctor of ministry degree in spirituality and spiritual leadership from the Chicago Theological Seminary. Pat is a member of the Sisters of Charity of the Blessed Virgin Mary of Dubuque, Iowa.

MARY PAT GANNON HAY graduated from Barat College of the Sacred Heart with a degree in political science and went on to work in local, state and national political campaigns. She worked in Mayor Harold Washington's press office as assistant press secretary and then in the private sector, working for Mesirow Financial. While at Mesirow, she became involved with Mercy Home for Boys and Girls, serving as the founding chair of its board of regents and then chairing the board of directors for eight years. She continues to serve on Mercy Home's board of directors. She is also on the board of directors for the Lyric Opera of Chicago and the advisory board of the School of Music for DePaul University.

WILLIAM ("BILL") E. HAY spent twelve years with Ernst & Young as Midwest regional head of executive search consulting. A native Chicagoan, Bill received a bachelor of business administration in management from the University of Illinois-Urbana and an MBA from DePaul University. After teaching full-time at DePaul for several years, he joined the adjunct faculty in the Graduate School of Business, the School of Public Service, and serves as advisor to the School for New Learning. In 2006, he and Mary Pat Hay received honorary degrees from the University's College of Liberal Arts and Sciences. Bill is a member of the board of trustees for DePaul University and of the board of directors of the Union League Club of Chicago, the Hope Institute for Children and Families, and the Career Transitions Center. Bill is also active with Mercy Home for Boys and Girls.

LIANNE HOWARD-DACE is community and events fundraising manager at the Royal London Society for the Blind in the UK; prior to that, she was Community Fundraiser at Depaul UK. An alumnus of the Depaul International Vincentian Values in Leadership initiative, Lianne is passionate about the values-based ethos of the Depaul Group and interested in the history of fundraising and Vincent de Paul's contribution to it. Lianne has recently completed the MSc Management in Civil Society program at London South Bank University.

BILL JASTER is co-director and co-founder (with Mary Frances) of CVV. He received an M.A. in adult Christian community development at Regis University, and a certificate in youth ministry from Mount St. Mary's University. Bill has been working in youth and young adult ministry since 1976. He is passionate about sharing the Vincentian spirit with others, which he has done with CVV from its inception in 1994.

MARY FRANCES JASTER is co-director and co-founder (with Bill) of Colorado Vincentian Volunteers (CVV), a program for young adults who want to immerse themselves in the Vincentian spirit through service in the Denver area. She holds a certificate in spiritual direction from St. Thomas Seminary (formerly staffed by Vincentians) and a master in intercultural relations from the University of the Pacific. She and her husband Bill are natives of Colorado and are parents of two grown children. Mary Frances' passion is to mentor young adults and to accompany them as spiritual director in their search for the spiritual connections in their work for the poor. She also loves being a grandmother.

Teresa Manna is the director of development for the Congregation of the Mission Western Province. In July 2004, under the leadership of the former Midwest Province, she established a comprehensive development program to support the many works of the Vincentian priests and brothers. The Province development office raised more than $18 million in contributions in the first ten years. Teresa's twenty-four years of development experience includes roles as the director of stewardship education and the director of the annual Catholic appeal for the Archdiocese of St. Louis. Teresa has served on several development committees and boards for nonprofit organizations in the St. Louis area. She has been an active member of the Association of Fundraising Professionals since 1998. Teresa is married with two children. She, her husband Lee, and their family are members of St. Clare of Assisi Catholic Church in Ellisville, Missouri.

Steven F. Martinez serves as National Development Director for the National Council of the U.S. Society of St. Vincent de Paul (SVdPUSA), located in Maryland Heights, Missouri. He has over 20 years of experience as a professional fundraiser. Since 2009, he has directed the national fundraising efforts at the Society, including the direct involvement of Vincentians from SVdP Conferences and Councils. SVdPUSA National programs include: National Vehicle Program, Friends of the Poor Walk, Friends of the Poor Grant Program, National Direct Mail Program, and other fundraising efforts to raise funds for the National Council.

MARK MCGREEVY is group chief executive at Depaul International, which coordinates the activities of a group of Depaul charities around the world, operating in the UK, Ireland, Slovakia, Ukraine, France, and the United States. Depaul's services offer support to homeless and disadvantaged people of all ages. Mark also provides pro bono consultancy to other voluntary sector organizations in the areas of corporate governance, strategic planning, and fundraising. He attended Ushaw College, Durham, in the UK where he trained for the priesthood 1980–85 (not ordained), followed by a degree at Durham University, 1984–87, and then a Post-Graduate Certificate in Voluntary Sector Management at Sheffield Hallam University. Before joining Depaul in 1990 as Services Manager, and becoming CEO in 1992, he worked and volunteered for other homelessness agencies in London.

J. PATRICK MURPHY, C.M., serves as values director of Depaul International, an organization serving the homeless in six countries. He founded Vincent on Leadership: The Hay Project, a research and training unit within DePaul University. Pat received a Ph.D. in higher education administration and an M.A. in sociology from Stanford, along with an MBA from DePaul. Pat writes and lectures internationally on leadership, values, and visioning for nonprofits. He is a Vincentian priest based in Chicago.

ROGER T. PLAYWIN specializes in strategic planning, organizational development, fundraising, government and public relations for nonprofits. He has assisted multiple nonprofits develop strategic organizational growth plans. Roger has a long history with nonprofits serving in a variety of roles including volunteer, staff, executive management, board member, committee chair, and elected officer. He is a trained process consultant and facilitator in change management and leadership development. Roger has worked in the for-profit, government, and nonprofit sectors. He served as a CEO for SVdPUSA for ten years. He recently retired and resides in Michigan.

MARK S. PRANAITIS, C.M., is a Vincentian priest serving as vice president of operations and advancement at the Association of Catholic Colleges and Universities in Washington, D.C. He is a trustee of DePaul University and has worked there previously. Mark earned a Ph.D. in organization development from Benedictine University. He provides consultation services to nonprofit organizations seeking to align governance and management structures with mission and improve their fundraising capacities.

JOHN E. RYBOLT, C.M., is the historian of the Congregation of the Mission, the Vincentians, currently finishing the sixth volume of The Vincentians. He initiated the Centre International de Formation (CIF), headquartered in Paris, France, designed for ongoing formation for members of the Congregation and the Vincentian Family. He holds several graduate degrees, including a Ph.D. in Biblical Studies from St. Louis University. As a Vincentian scholar-in-residence at DePaul University, he resides in Chicago.

CHARLES F. SHELBY, C.M., is a vice chancellor at DePaul University. His duties are university-wide and include promoting the Vincentian and Catholic mission of the university, public relations, alumni relations, fundraising, and correspondence. He is a priest of the Congregation of the Mission of Saint Vincent de Paul, the Vincentians, who sponsor DePaul University. He has a master of divinity from DeAndreis Seminary in Lemont, Illinois, and a master of science in physics from DePaul University. Charles served on the board of directors of the National Catholic Development Conference for nine years, serving as board chair and vice chair. From 1983 to June 30, 2005, he served as director and president of the Association of the Miraculous Medal in Perryville, Missouri.

Made in the USA
Columbia, SC
05 August 2018